BACK
IN THE
DAY

TRIVIA FOR SENIORS

Facts and Trivia from History and
Pop Culture to Keep Your Mind Sharp
and Boost Your Memory

ANDREW THOMPSON

Published by:
Ulysses Press
PO Box 3440
Berkeley, CA 94703
www.ulyssespress.com

ISBN: 978-1-64604-446-7
Library of Congress Control Number: 2022944117

Printed in the United States by Versa Press
10 9 8 7 6 5 4 3 2 1

Acquisitions editor: Claire Sielaff
Managing editor: Claire Chun
Project editor: Melody Gallozo
Editor: Scott Calamar
Proofreader: Renee Rutledge
Front cover design: Rebecca Lown
Production: Winnie Liu
Cover and interior images: from shutterstock.com—boom box © Vectorcarrot; corvette © DMaryashin; couple dancing, greaser © RetroClipArt; disco ball © m2art; movie project © Sergii Tverdokhlibov; peace sign © MeSamongeps; roller skates © LHF Graphics; trumpet player © KUCO; TV © Viktorus

CONTENTS

INTRODUCTION 1

1950s: THE GOLDEN AGE 3

HIGH SOCIETY

Greasers................................. 3
Bikinis and Stilettos 4
The Need for Speed...................... 4
Let's Drive 4

Montgomery Bus Boycott 5
Baby Boomers................................. 5
The Law of Averages.......................... 5

IT'S A POLITICAL THING

Apartheid in South Africa 6
The Korean War................................ 6
Two Terms 6
Libyan Independence.......................... 6
Queen Elizabeth II 6
Stalin....................................... 7
The Algerian War 7

Princess Grace 7
The Suez Crisis 7
The ECC.......................... 7
China's Great Leap Forward............ 8
The Cuban Revolution 8
And Then There Were Fifty 8

A SCIENTIFIC WORLD

Transistor Radios............................. 8
The Hydrogen Bomb 8
The Structure of DNA 9
Nuclear Power................................. 9

Polio Vaccine 9
Einstein.. 9
Sputnik 1 and *2* 9

MUSIC AND THE ARTS

Peanuts 10
The Crooners................................ 10
The Catcher in the Rye 10
The Old Man and the Sea 10
Hank Williams 11
The King Is Crowned......................... 11
The Million-Dollar Quartet............... 11

Jackson Pollock............................ 12
Dr. Seuss.................................... 12
On the Road............................... 12
The Day the Music Died................... 12
The Biggest Sellers in Music............ 12

A SPORTING LIFE

Formula One Begins................13
Farewell to the Yankee Clipper........13
Helsinki Olympics................13
Rocky................13
Mount Everest Scaled 14
The Four-Minute Mile...................14
Pelé Emerges.......................14
The Great American Pastime..........14
The Lakers.................15
Hut Hut!...........15

THE BIG (AND SMALL) SCREEN

It's in Color....................15
I Love Lucy...............................15
Adventures of Superman.....................15
Marilyn and Joe.................16
Miss America.......................16
The $64,000 Question 16
Rebel Without a Cause 17
The Golden Age of Television...........17
Bigger than Ben-Hur....................17
Rawhide 17

IT'S JUST BUSINESS

Put It on Credit................. 18
The Bar Code 18
Mr. Potato Head 18
No-Cal.................. 18
Disneyland.......................19
Let's Go Shopping.............................19
NASA Is Born 19
Hula Hoops 20
I'm a Barbie Girl... 20
The Rich List.................... 20

IN INFAMY

Ten Most Wanted........................... 20
Chinchaga Fire.......................21
Assassination Attempt.....................21
Earthquake 21
Children of Thalidomide 21
Midair Disaster.......................21
Hurricane Audrey 22

THE WEIRD AND THE WONDERFUL

Telephone Booth Stuffing 22
Conical Bras 22
Fuzzy Dice.......................22

POP QUIZ HOT SHOT.. 23

1960s: THE SWINGING SIXTIES................ 25

HIGH SOCIETY

Mop Tops and Miniskirts................25
Growth.................26
Flower Power.......................26
Women's Liberation 26
Woodstock.................... 27
Generation X.................... 27
Decline in Farming.................... 27
Crime on the Rise...........................28
The Law of Averages 28

IT'S A POLITICAL THING

Bay of Pigs.............................28
The Berlin Wall......................28
Independence for Algeria...............29
Cuban Missile Crisis 29
I Have a Dream 29
African Unity...............................30
Mandela Jailed...............................30
Vietnam 30
Revolution in China 30
The Troubles in Ireland.....................31
France Strikes 31
Invasion of Czechoslovakia...............31
The Stonewall Riots 31
Gaddafi to Power 32

A SCIENTIFIC WORLD

Inventions 32
Bombs Away...............................32
The Pill 32
Unimate....................................33
First Man in Space.........................33
Telstar 1 33
Touch-Tone Dialing.......................33
The Big Bang 33
The Space Race Goes On...............33
Heart Transplant 34
One Small Step.............................34
Concorde....................................34

MUSIC AND THE ARTS

The End of Rock (for Now).............34
The Rat Pack 35
Ernest Hemingway Dies.................35
Beatlemania................................35
Bob Dylan....................................35
Surf Rock....................................36
The Man in Black 36
The King Is Back............................36
Andy Warhol Shot 36
Literature Booms 36
Jack Kerouac Dies.........................37

A SPORTING LIFE

Olympics 37
I Am the Greatest! 37
Baseball's Expansion 38
The Celtics...................................38
Green Bay 38

THE BIG (AND SMALL) SCREEN

The Flintstones 38
Marilyn Dies................................39
The Man with No Name..................39
The Sound of Music.......................39
ZAP! POW! 39
Walt Disney Dies 40
Easy Rider....................................40
The Brady Bunch 40

IT'S JUST BUSINESS

Wall Street...............................40
The Chain Store 41
Nike 41
High-Speed Rail............................41
Cars, Cars, Cars 41
Automated Banking.........................41
The Gap 42
A Tobacco Change.........................42

IN INFAMY

Valdivia Earthquake 42
Midair Disaster................................42
Escape from Alcatraz.......................43
President Kennedy Assassinated 43
Malcolm X 43

Che Guevara Killed..........................44
Martin Luther King Jr.
Assassinated 44
Robert Kennedy Killed 44
Manson Murders..............................44

THE WEIRD AND THE WONDERFUL

Breast Implants 45
Smiley Face 45

Lava Lamps 45
Tie-Dye..45

POP QUIZ HOT SHOT...46

1970s: THE ME DECADE 47

HIGH SOCIETY

Women in the Workforce.............. 48
Bell-Bottoms and Farrah Hair 48
Earth Day 48
Right to Vote.................................. 48

Reduced Growth.............................49
Generation X Continues.................49
The Law of Averages.......................49

IT'S A POLITICAL THING

Quebec Problems 50
Idi Amin 50
Nixon and Mao.............................. 50
Philippines under Martial Law........ 50
Bloody Sunday 50
Chilean Coup 51
Yom Kippur 51
Invasion of Cyprus 51
Vietnam Over 51
Further African Decolonization.......51
Civil War in Lebanon.......................52

Pol Pot...52
Western Sahara War 52
Protests in South Africa.................52
Death of Mao Zedong 53
Coup in Argentina 53
Year of Three Popes 53
Russians in Afghanistan..................53
Margaret Thatcher..........................54
Oil Crisis...54
Saddam Hussein to Power..............54

A SCIENTIFIC WORLD

Pocket Calculators..........................54
Intel 4004 54
You Have Mail 55
Video Games..................................55
Floppy Disks...................................55

Last Man on the Moon 55
VCRs Available 55
First MRI...55
Cell Phones 56
Genetic Engineering.......................56

Lucy 56
IVF First 56
Smallpox Eradicated 57

Microwave Ovens 57
Voicemail Begins..........................57

MUSIC AND THE ARTS
Buy the Ticket, Take the Ride 57
Eagles................................57
The Twenty-Seven Club 58
Hot August Night...................58
The Dark Side of the Moon...................58
Piano Man 58
Stephen King....................................59

Motown 59
Disco.......................................59
Rock..59
Punk Rock 59
Outlaws..60
The King Is Dead 60
Led Zeppelin and Elton John..........60

A SPORTING LIFE
Olympics 60
Dolphins Go All the Way..................61
The Rumble in the Jungle.................61
Nadia....................................61

Tennis....................................62
The Athletics, the Reds, and
the Yankees......................................62
Basketball Spirit 62

THE BIG (AND SMALL) SCREEN
All in the Family 63
Adult Entertainment 63
Bruce Lee Dies............................63
The Godfather 63
Happy Days.....................................63

Rocky....................................64
Star Wars.......................................64
Dallas...64
Superman......................................64
Female Leads..................................65

IT'S JUST BUSINESS
Amtrak Formed...............................65
Evel Knievel Toy 65
Magnavox Odyssey..........................65
Japanese Cars................................66
Sears Tower.....................................66

Microsoft 66
Apple.......................................66
Atari 66
Space Invaders..............................67
The First Walkman 67

IN INFAMY
Palestinian Hijackings.....................67
Cyclone in Pakistan 67
Genocide in Bangladesh 68
Capital Punishment 68
Super Outbreak 68
Watergate.......................................68

Emperor of Ethiopia
Assassinated 69
President of Bangladesh
Assassinated 69
SS Edmund Fitzgerald 69
President Ford Assassination
Attempts 69

Tenerife Airport Disaster................70   American Airlines Flight 191 70
Jonestown...70   Three Mile Island.............................70

THE WEIRD AND THE WONDERFUL

The Disco Ball 71   Pet Rocks 71
Platform Shoes................................71   Mohawk Hair.....................................71

POP QUIZ HOT SHOT..72

1980s: THE GREED DECADE 73

HIGH SOCIETY

Walkmans and Boom Boxes 74   Generation Y.....................................74
Big Hair and Acid-Washed Jeans....74   The Law of Averages.......................74

IT'S A POLITICAL THING

Reagan to Power..............................75   Grenada Invaded 76
Iran-Iraq War....................................75   Civil War in Sri Lanka......................76
Mugabe to Power.............................75   British Miners' Strike.......................77
Operation Opera 75   Brazilian Democracy........................77
The Falklands....................................76   The Wall Falls...................................77
Independence from Britain 76   Tiananmen Square............................77
Lebanon Invaded 76

A SCIENTIFIC WORLD

Voyager..78   Camcorders......................................79
Space Shuttle 78   Halley's Comet 79
The CD 78   Surrogate Pregnancies....................79
Artificial Heart.................................78   Prozac 79
Home Computers.............................79   Designer Babies 79

MUSIC AND THE ARTS

The Eighties.....................................80   Like a Virgin......................................81
Lennon Dies (As Do Others).........80   Born in the USA................................81
MTV..80   Hard Rock and Heavy Metal..........82
Queen..80   Live Aid..82
Thriller..81   Hip-Hop 82
Purple Rain..81   Best-Selling Books...........................82

A SPORTING LIFE

Gretsky 82
WrestleMania 83
The Bear Is Back 83
The Goal of the Century 83
Magic and Bird 83

Olympics 84
World Series Firsts................84
The 49ers and the Redskins...........85
Tennis 85

THE BIG (AND SMALL) SCREEN

Magnum PI............................85
Prime-Time Soaps...........................86
The Smurfs............................86
E.T. the Extra-Terrestrial......................86
Letterman..............................86
Cable TV................................86

The Brat Pack....................87
The Blockbuster 87
Action Franchises 87
Television Sitcoms...........87
Martial Arts Films 88
The Oscars....................... 88

IT'S JUST BUSINESS

Rubik's Cube 88
Pac-Man 88
Wayfarers and Aviators...................89
Swatches...............................89
Black Monday.............................89
Apple Mac 89

Microsoft Windows..........................89
Hyundai 89
Disposable Camera 90
The Richest........................ 90
Gameboy 90

IN INFAMY

Mount St. Helens Erupts 90
President Reagan Attacked............ 90
Attempt on the Pope......................91
Egyptian President Killed 91
AIDS 91
Korean Air Lines Flight 007 91
Famine in Ethiopia 92
Indira Gandhi Assassination 92
Japan Airlines Flight Crash 92

Air India Flight 182 92
Challenger Explodes......................92
Chernobyl................................93
Lockerbie Bombing.........................93
Drought 93
Iran Air Flight 655.......................93
Oil Spill..................................93
Loma Prieta Earthquake.................94

THE WEIRD AND THE WONDERFUL

Yo-Yos Are Back............................94
The Mullet 94
Valspeak....................................94

Cabbage Patch Kids........................95
Car Surfing.................................95
Hacky Sacks 95

POP QUIZ HOT SHOT

POP QUIZ HOT SHOT..96

1990s: THE GOOD DECADE.............. 97

HIGH SOCIETY

Year of the Woman 98
Global Warming 98
Flannels and Curtained Hair 98
Growth..98
Generation Z 99
The Law of Averages 99

IT'S A POLITICAL THING

Gulf War 99
Nelson Mandela 99
Soviet Union Ends 100
War in Yugoslavia 100
European Union 101
Oslo Accords....................................101
Massacre in Rwanda........................101
Haiti Invasion...................................101
Chechen War 101
Cannabis Legalized..........................102
Congo Wars......................................102
Hong Kong Back to China.............102
Clinton and Lewinsky 102
The Kosovo War 102
Irish Peace 102
Putin Leads Russia 103

A SCIENTIFIC WORLD

World Wide Web..............................103
Hubble 103
Mummy Found..................................103
GPS..103
International Space Station...........104
Genetically Modified Foods..........104
DVDs..104
Hello, Dolly 104
Pathfinder...104
Instant Messenger 104
MP3 Players......................................105
Camera Phones................................105

MUSIC AND THE ARTS

Friends in Low Places.....................105
Grunge...105
Alternative Rock 106
The Firm...106
Gangsta Rap 106
Jagged Little Pill 106
Rap Artists Killed 106
Versace Murdered.......................... 107
Harry Potter..................................... 107
John Denver Dies 107
Goodbye, Frank 107
Pop Music..108
Mariah..108

A SPORTING LIFE

Atlanta Braves.................................108
Air Jordan...108
Olympics 109
The Cowboys and the Broncos.......110
Baseball Strike.................................110
Formula One 110
Brazil Takes Four 110
Iron Mike Takes a Bite 110
Lance Armstrong 111
Tennis.. 111

THE BIG (AND SMALL) SCREEN

The Simpsons 111
Teen Soaps 112
Legal Dramas 112
Seinfeld 112
River Phoenix Dies 112
Cheers 112
Medical Dramas 113
Cult Following 113
Toy Story and Animation 113
Titanic 113
Baywatch 113
Academy Awards 113

IT'S JUST BUSINESS

Ronald in Russia 114
The Hummer 114
The Super Soaker 114
Channel Tunnel 114
PlayStation 114
Barings Bank Collapses 115
E-Commerce 115
Hotmail 115
Netflix 115
The Tallest 115
Google 115
iMac 116

IN INFAMY

LA Riots 116
Columbus Day 116
Hurricane Andrew 116
Sicilian Mafia 116
World Trade Center Bombing 117
Escobar Killed 117
The Waco Siege 117
Rwandan Plane Shot Down 117
Oklahoma Bombing 118
O. J. Simpson 118
Midwestern Heat Wave 118
Trans World Airlines Flight 118
Unabomber Arrested 118
The Taliban 119
Princess Diana Dies 119
Mother Teresa Dies 119
Earthquakes in Turkey 119
JFK Jr. Killed 119

THE WEIRD AND THE WONDERFUL

Slap Bracelets 120
Lorena Bobbitt 120
Wonderbra 120
Y2K Fears 120

POP QUIZ HOT SHOT
POP QUIZ HOT SHOT 121

2000s: THE NOUGHTIES
2000s: THE NOUGHTIES 123

HIGH SOCIETY

Millennium Madness 124
Growth 124
Generation Z Continues 124
A Technological World 125
The Law of Averages 125

IT'S A POLITICAL THING

George W. Bush Elected 125
Netherlands Same-Sex
Marriage 125
Twin Towers Fall....................... 125
War in Iraq 126
The Sudan 126
Reagan Dies 126

Mexican Drug War.......................127
North Korea Goes Nuclear 127
Kosovo Independent 127
Obama Becomes President...........127
South Ossetia War..........................127
Global Warming 128

A SCIENTIFIC WORLD

International Space Station...........128
Artificial Heart........................... 128
Space Tourism 128

Mars Exploration Rover................. 128
Pluto Demoted 129
Large Hadron Collider 129

MUSIC AND THE ARTS

The Da Vinci Code 129
Simon and Garfunkel Return 129
The Man in Black Departs 129
Hunter S. Thompson.......................130
Rolling Stones Go Big....................130
Hip-Hop 130

R&B 130
Music Artist of the Decade...........130
Drawing by Raphael....................... 131
Goodbye, Michael Jackson
(and Others) 131

A SPORTING LIFE

Olympics 131
Tiger Wins Three 132
Lakers Three-Peat........................ 132
Beckham Comes to America 133

The Yankees Start and Finish 133
Steelers Record.............................. 133
Ronaldo Record 133
Federer 133

THE BIG (AND SMALL) SCREEN

Reality Television............................134
Drama Series..................................134
Comedy Continues........................134
Gladiator Wins................................135
Shrek and Computer
Animation.......................................135

Prime-Time Soaps.......................... 135
Lord of the Rings............................. 135
Fahrenheit 9/11.............................. 135
Avatar 136
Superheroes Are Back................... 136
Time to Switch Off 136

IT'S JUST BUSINESS

PlayStation 2.................................. 136
Segway...137
Xbox 137
Websites Soar.................................137

Collapse of Enron 137
The Dot-Com Bubble Bursts.........137
AOL and Warner............................137
iPod 138

Birth of the Euro 138
Concorde Grounded 138
Nokia's Rise and Fall 138
Google Floats 138
Facebook 138
Nintendo DS 139
YouTube 139
Wii Sports 139

Twitter 139
iPhone 139
MacBook Air 139
Bernie Madoff 140
Bull Market 140
Economic Crisis 140
WhatsApp 140
Bill Still on Top 140

IN INFAMY

Anthrax Attacks 141
American Airlines Flight 587 141
Earthquake in Gujarat 141
Milošević on Trial 141
Terrorist Attacks 142
Space Shuttle Columbia 142

Tsunami 142
Beslan Hostage Crisis 142
Katrina 143
George Tiller Killed 143
Swine Flu 143

THE WEIRD AND THE WONDERFUL

Janet at the Super Bowl 143

Geek Chic 144

POP QUIZ HOT SHOT 145

2010s: THE TEN-SIONS 147

HIGH SOCIETY

Hipsters and Active Wear 148
Decline in Growth 148

Generation Alpha 148
The Law of Averages 149

IT'S A POLITICAL THING

Bin Laden Killed 149
Arab Spring 149
Libya 149
Occupy Wall Street 150
Syrian War 150
Nelson Mandela Dies 150
Black Lives Matter 150
Russia in Ukraine 150
Hong Kong Protests 150
Islamic State 151
Obergefell v. Hodges 151

Trump Elected 151
Turkey Invades Syria 152
Brexit 152
Castro Dies 152
Philippine Drug War 152
Nuclear Reduction 152
Mugabe Gone 153
Women March 153
Yellow Vests Protests 153
Korean Leaders Meet 153
George Bush Dies 153

Chinese Leader for Life 154
India and Pakistan 154
Persian Gulf Crisis 154

Trump to North Korea 154
Trump Impeached 155

A SCIENTIFIC WORLD

Drones 155
Mobile Apps 155
The Shuttle Is Grounded 155
Curiosity 155
China Goes to the Moon...............156

3D Printers....................................156
Electric Cars..................................156
Event Horizon Telescope..............156
5G 156

MUSIC AND THE ARTS

Country Music Resurgence 157
Streaming Music 157
Pop Music......................................157
Rock Revival..................................157

Artist of the Decade......................157
Best-Selling Books........................158
Whitney and Others......................158

A SPORTING LIFE

Kelly Slater Keeps on Winning......158
Olympics 158
Armstrong Stripped 159
The Cubs Win................................159
Goodbye, Ali 159

Golden State Warriors...................160
New England Patriots Win
Three..160
Tennis...160

THE BIG (AND SMALL) SCREEN

Online Streaming...........................161
Animated Films..............................161
It...161
Superheroes 161
Joker..162
Reality TV......................................162

Best Picture...................................162
Drama Series.................................162
The Big Bang Theory 162
Robin Williams and Others
Depart...163

IT'S JUST BUSINESS

iPad 163
Bitcoin and Cryptocurrency 163
Instagram.......................................164
Goodbye, Steve Jobs 164
Murdoch and News of the
World 164

Google Chrome 164
Amazon Echo 164
Playboy Hugh Bows Out...............164
Cashless Society 165
Minecraft.......................................165

IN INFAMY

Volcano in Iceland 165
Deepwater Horizon 165
Haiti Earthquake 166
Earthquake in Chile 166
Chilean Miners 166
Super Outbreak 166
Drought in California 166
Tucson Shooting 167
Tsunami in Japan 167
Shootings at Sandy Hook 167
Meteor in Russia 167
Malaysia Airlines Flight 370 167

Stampede in Mina 168
Data Breach 168
CBS Murders 168
Fox News Scandal 168
Hurricane Harvey 168
Weinstein 169
Thailand Cave Rescue 169
California Camp Fire 169
Notre-Dame Burns 170
Terrorism Continues 170
COVID-19 170

THE WEIRD AND THE WONDERFUL

Fedoras Are Back 171
Selfie Sticks 171
Dabbing 171

Emojis 171
Fidget Spinner 171

POP QUIZ HOT SHOT 172

ABOUT THE AUTHOR 175

INTRODUCTION

Where were you when you first heard an Elvis Presley song? Where were you when man first landed on the moon? Where were you when the Watergate scandal broke? Where were you when the Berlin Wall fell? Where were you when Nelson Mandela was released from jail? Where were you when the Twin Towers were hit? Where were you when Usain Bolt set the world record for 100 meters?

And then there's one of the most famous "where were you whens?" of them all—Where were you when you heard the news that JFK had been shot?

Back in the Day Trivia for Seniors takes you on a journey through seven decades of fascinating facts, covering topics such as politics, science, music and the arts, business, sports, film and television, cultural trends, the infamous, as well as the weird and the wonderful.

From the "Golden Age" of the 1950s all the way through to the modern era, you will be taken on a nostalgic journey down memory lane.

Set up in easy-to-digest categories, with bite-size facts and snapshots from history, *Back in the Day Trivia for Seniors* is a book that you can dip in and out of, or read from cover to cover. From the birth of rock 'n' roll to modern pop, from the Korean War to the "war on terror," from the baby boomers to Generation Alpha, this book will make you feel as if you're traveling back in time. And to test your memory, there's a short quiz at the end of each decade.

So sit back and relax, cast your mind to back in the day, and enjoy the ride.

1950s

THE GOLDEN AGE

The 1950s were known as the "Golden Age" of America and saw the world continue its recovery from World War II. At the same time, the Cold War between the United States and the Soviet Union intensified. The battle between capitalism and communism resulted in a number of conflicts, such as the Korean War and the Cuban Revolution, and spurred the start of the space race between the two global giants, as well as the increased development of nuclear weapons. The United States emerged as the most powerful economic country in the world under President Dwight D. Eisenhower. And as world economies expanded throughout the decade, so did populations, as the so-called baby boomer generation emerged to usher in the second half of the twentieth century.

HIGH SOCIETY

Greasers

1950   The 1950s saw the establishment of greasers in the United States, with many young men, who previously dressed like their parents, wearing leather jackets, tight jeans, and boots, with slicked back, greasy hair. The trend was thought to be largely influenced by the character played by Marlon Brando in the 1953 film *The Wild One*.

Bikinis and Stilettos

1950   At the same time as the greasers, the bikini gained in popularity, promoted by Hollywood stars such as Ava Gardner, Rita Hayworth, Elizabeth Taylor, and Marilyn Monroe. In 1950, Elvira Pagã walked in a golden bikini at the Rio Carnival, starting a tradition at the event. Stiletto heels (named after the stiletto dagger) also gained popularity in the 1950s in France, and they quickly spread to the United States.

The Need for Speed

1953   By the mid-1950s, American society had developed a taste for speed. The world was getting faster and the people wanted to move with it. Ready meals were developed to be made quickly at home, and in 1953 Swanson marketed "TV dinners." In that year alone, over seventy million TV dinners were sold in the United States, the first one being a Thanksgiving-inspired meal of turkey, stuffing, sweet potato, and peas. And while the McDonald's hamburger chain began in the 1940s, the franchise started under Ray Kroc in 1955, when its first burgers were sold for fifteen cents each. In 1950, Kraft produced packaged cheese slices.

Let's Drive

1954   As Americans moved out of the cities and to the suburbs during the 1950s, the society was transformed and people needed a means to move around, with limited public transport available. By 1954, the country boasted 47 million cars, and 80 percent of American families owned at least one car. Most cars were American made, and like the Cadillac, were large and designed for style as opposed to convenience. In 1956, President Eisenhower signed the Federal-Aid Highway Act to create 41,000 miles of national highways.

Montgomery Bus Boycott

1955   In Montgomery, Alabama, a Black woman named Rosa Parks refused to obey the law and give up her seat to a white person. She was jailed, and this led to a boycott of the bus system by the Black population, eventually ending segregation on Montgomery's buses. The boycott lasted 381 days and was overseen by Martin Luther King Jr., the tension of the situation leading to his house being bombed. King was arrested and jailed during the campaign, and his role propelled him into an influential national figure and champion of the Civil Rights Movement. This followed the 1954 US Supreme Court ruling in *Brown v. Board of Education of Topeka* that separate schools for Black and white children were unconstitutional.

Baby Boomers

1957   The 1950s were known for population growth, with a generation called the "baby boomers." This peaked in 1957, when just under 4.3 million babies were born in the United States. In 1950, the population of the United States was around 151 million and the world population was around 2.6 billion.

The Law of Averages

1959   In 1950, the average home in the United States cost $7,354. By the end of the decade, the cost had risen to $11,900. The average family income rose from $3,300 in 1950 to $5,400 in 1959, while the average price of a gallon of gas rose from 27 cents in 1950 to 30 cents in 1959. The minimum wage in 1950 was 75 cents an hour.

Apartheid in South Africa

1950   After launching a policy of racial segregation known as apartheid in 1948, the African National Congress party began rebelling against the laws, leading to violent clashes across the country.

The Korean War

1950   The conflict, which lasted from 1950 to 1953, began as a civil war between North and South Korea for control over the Korean peninsula, but it quickly escalated to a global conflict, with the United States and its allies supporting South Korea against the Soviet Union and China. More than 33,000 American soldiers died in the war, while Korean and Chinese casualties numbered more than one million.

Two Terms

1951   The Twenty-Second Amendment was ratified in February 1951, meaning US presidents were officially limited to two terms in power.

Libyan Independence

1951   The 1950s saw the decolonization of Africa, with Libya the first country to gain independence in 1951. Sudan, Morocco, and Tunisia achieved the same result in 1956, and Ghana followed in 1957 when it gained independence from the British Empire.

Queen Elizabeth II

1952   After the death of her father, King George VI, Elizabeth became the queen of the United Kingdom, a position she would hold for at least seventy years.

Stalin

1953   Generally considered to be one of the most influential figures of the twentieth century, Joseph Stalin died in March 1953. His totalitarian regime has been universally condemned for overseeing widespread ethnic cleansing. His death began a phase of bitter power struggles in the Soviet Union.

The Algerian War

1954   Lasting from 1954 until 1962, this war was fought by the Algerians to gain independence from its French colonizers, something they eventually achieved.

Princess Grace

1956   American actress Grace Kelly became princess of Monaco when she married Prince Rainier III in April of 1956. Kelly died at the age of fifty-two from injuries sustained in a car crash in 1982.

The Suez Crisis

1956   After the Suez Canal was nationalized by the Egyptians, the United Kingdom, France, and Israel invaded Egypt but were forced to withdraw after the United States and the Soviet Union united in opposition. This was a key moment in the end of European global power.

The ECC

1957   The European Economic Community was established in 1957, aimed at setting up a common market. It began with six countries— France, Italy, Germany, Belgium, the Netherlands, and Luxembourg— and was the forerunner for the European Union.

China's Great Leap Forward

1958   Led by Mao Zedong, a program known as the "Great Leap Forward" sought to change the country from a rural to an industrial economy, forcing people to produce steel rather than food. The policy was disastrous and resulted in widespread famine and the death of an estimated 35 million Chinese.

The Cuban Revolution

1959   After a six-year battle, Cuban revolutionaries led by Fidel Castro and the Argentinian-born Ernesto "Che" Guevara overthrew the dictator Fulgencio Batista to create a communist government, which Castro led until 2008.

And Then There Were Fifty

1959   In January 1959, Alaska became the forty-ninth state in the United States. Then in August, Hawaii became the fiftieth.

A SCIENTIFIC WORLD

Transistor Radios

1951   The first commercial production of the transistor radio began in Allentown, Pennsylvania, leading to the success of the portable radio by 1954.

The Hydrogen Bomb

1952   Seven years after Hiroshima, the United States conducted the first test of a hydrogen, or thermonuclear, bomb. Code named "Ivy Mike," the mushroom cloud from the explosion rose to an altitude of 56,000 feet in ninety seconds, before spreading out to a diameter of one hundred miles. The bomb destroyed the Pacific island where it was detonated.

The Structure of DNA

1953   Scientists James Watson and Francis Crick discovered the double-helix structure of DNA (deoxyribonucleic acid), the molecule found in every cell. DNA profiling was developed in 1984 by Alec Jeffreys, the British geneticist, and was first used in 1988 to convict Colin Pitchfork of murder.

Nuclear Power

1954   The world's first nuclear power plant was built in Obninsk in the Soviet Union.

Polio Vaccine

1955   Jonas Salk, the American virologist, developed the first successful polio vaccine, which was given to over seven million Americas. This was instrumental in reducing the number of worldwide cases from around 350,000 in 1988 to just thirty-three in 2018.

Einstein

1955   Albert Einstein, the German-born theoretical physicist, died in April of 1955 in New Jersey at the age of seventy-six. Widely regarded as one of the greatest physicists of all time, Einstein is best known for developing the theory of relativity.

Sputnik 1 and 2

1957   The Soviet Union launched the first artificial satellite into Earth's orbit, taking an early lead in the space race. It was named *Sputnik 1* and weighed only 184 pounds. Later that same year, *Sputnik 2* carried the first living creature into space—a dog named Laika. Laika was a stray mongrel from the streets of Moscow. She was the first animal to orbit the Earth but died of overheating within hours. The truth about her death was not revealed until 2002.

Peanuts

1950   The daily and Sunday American comic strip written and illustrated by Charles M. Schulz was first published in 1950 and continues to this day. The most popular comic strip of all time, nearly 18,000 strips have been published. *Peanuts* has run in over 2,600 newspapers with a readership of over 350 million.

The Crooners

1950   The decade began the same as the prior one ended, with the most popular music being the sounds of crooners such as Frank Sinatra, who eventually sold an estimated 150 million records worldwide.

The Catcher in the Rye

1951   J. D. Salinger sprang to fame with the popular success of his book *The Catcher in the Rye*. Salinger's depiction of adolescence in the novel was considered controversial at the time, leading him to become reclusive. He then published infrequently until his death in 2010.

The Old Man and the Sea

1952   The most famous of Ernest Hemingway's books, *The Old Man and the Sea* tells the story of Santiago, an old Cuban fisherman who struggles after hooking a giant marlin in the Gulf Stream. The book was awarded the Pulitzer Prize in 1953 and was instrumental in Hemingway receiving the Nobel Prize in Literature in 1954.

Hank Williams

1953   Arguably the most influential country music singer of all time, Hank Williams died of a heart attack while riding as a passenger in a car in West Virginia on January 1, 1953. He was only twenty-nine years old. With hits such as "Lovesick Blues," "Your Cheatin' Heart," "Hey Good Lookin'," and "I'm So Lonesome I Could Cry," Williams was inducted into the Country Music Hall of Fame in 1961.

The King Is Crowned

1954   The "King of Rock 'n' Roll," Elvis Presley released his first single, "That's All Right (Mama)" in 1954. He would go on to sell more than 500 million records worldwide by his death in 1977 and is recognized by Guinness World Records as the best-selling solo music artist of all time. But it was Alan Freed, a radio DJ in Cleveland, Ohio, who first coined the name "rock 'n' roll" to describe the emerging popular music genre in 1951.

The Million-Dollar Quartet

1956   An impromptu jam session at Sun Record Studios in Memphis, Tennessee, saw Elvis Presley, Johnny Cash, Jerry Lee Lewis, and Carl Perkins collaborate. All signed by the record producer Sam Phillips, the quartet was photographed by George Pierce, and the photo and an article appeared in the *Memphis Press-Scimitar* newspaper. The photo became famous, and the rest, as they say, is history.

Jackson Pollock

1956   The famous American painter Jackson Pollock, a major figure in the abstract expressionist movement, died in a car crash while driving under the influence of alcohol.

Dr. Seuss

1957   The landmark book *The Cat in the Hat* was published in 1957 by Theodor Geisel, the American writer better known as Dr. Seuss. After three years in print, the book had sold nearly one million copies, and it has now sold more than ten million copies.

On the Road

1957   Beatnik writer Jack Kerouac found fame with his 1957 novel based on his travels across the United States. Considered a defining work of the counterculture generation, it has been cited as an influence on various writers and musicians such as Hunter S. Thompson and Bob Dylan.

The Day the Music Died

1959   On a cold and blustery February night in 1959, a chartered plane crashed near Clear Lake, Iowa, killing all four people on board, including Ritchie Valens, J. P. "The Big Bopper" Richardson, and Buddy Holly. The tragedy was popularized by Don McLean's 1972 song "American Pie." Waylon Jennings, the famous American country singer, who was working with Holly as a bass player, originally had a seat on the plane, but gave it up at the last minute and lived until 2002.

The Biggest Sellers in Music

1959   Elvis Presley was the biggest-selling music artist of the decade, followed by Frank Sinatra. But the biggest-selling single was

"Rock around the Clock" by Bill Haley & His Comets, which was released in 1955. It sold almost 1.4 million copies.

A SPORTING LIFE

Formula One Begins

1950   The inaugural season of Formula One began, with the first world championship race taking place at Silverstone in the United Kingdom. Giuseppe Farina won the first World Drivers' Championship in 1950, his Alfa Romeo defeating his teammate Juan Manuel Fangio. Fangio then went on to win the title five times in the 1950s, a record that stood until 2003, when Michael Schumacher won his sixth title.

Farewell to the Yankee Clipper

1951   Joe DiMaggio retired from baseball after the 1951 season, ranking fifth at the time in career home runs. Inducted into the Baseball Hall of Fame in 1955, he was later voted baseball's greatest living player.

Helsinki Olympics

1952   The 1952 Olympics held in Helsinki, Finland, saw the Soviet Union participating for the first time, coming in second to the United States. These games saw the most world records broken, a record held until the 2008 Olympics in Beijing. The next Olympics, held in Melbourne, Australia, in 1956, were won by the Soviet Union, closely followed by the United States, with the host country coming in third.

Rocky

1952   Rocky Marciano faced Jersey Joe Walcott in 1952 for his first heavyweight title fight. Marciano knocked out the champion and became the world heavyweight champion for the first time at age twenty-nine. Marciano went on to defend his title a number of times before announcing his retirement in 1956, at just thirty-two years of age. He is the only heavyweight champion to have finished his career undefeated, with a record of 49–0. Marciano died in a plane crash in 1969, aged forty-five.

Mount Everest Scaled

1953   The highest mountain in the world was climbed for the first time by the New Zealand mountaineer and beekeeper Edmund Hillary. It has now been successfully climbed by more than four thousand people, while over three hundred people have perished in the attempt.

The Four-Minute Mile

1954   In 1954, Roger Bannister, the English middle-distance runner, became the first person to run a mile in under four minutes. Unfortunately for him, the record only lasted forty-six days, when his Australian rival, John Landy, went faster.

Pelé Emerges

1958   The 1958 soccer World Cup saw Pelé compete as the youngest person to play in a World Cup at age seventeen. He scored two goals, as Brazil beat Sweden 5–2. He was awarded the second-best player of the tournament. He is the only player to have won the World Cup three times, and his 1,279 goals in 1,363 games is a Guinness World Record.

The Great American Pastime

1959   The Yankees continued their dominance in the 1950s, winning six World Series in the decade and competing in eight of the ten finals. All six were managed by Casey Stengel, who was elected to the Baseball Hall of Fame in 1966.

The Lakers

1959 The Minneapolis Lakers played in five NBA Finals during the 1950s, winning four of them. They were then relocated to Los Angeles for the 1960 season.

Hut Hut!

1959 The Cleveland Browns played in seven of the ten NFL championships during the decade but only won three of them. And it was in 1950 that football games were televised for the first time.

THE BIG (AND SMALL) SCREEN

It's in Color

1951 Color television was first broadcast in the United States in 1951, but it was hard to get a hold of a color set, with the government banning their sale to conserve materials for the Korean War effort.

I Love Lucy

1951 One of the most successful sitcoms of all time, *I Love Lucy* debuted in 1951, with 180 episodes airing during its six seasons.

Adventures of Superman

1952 With 104 episodes that ran from 1952 to 1958, *Adventures of Superman* was an American television series based on the comic book created in 1938. George Reeves played the title character with the first two seasons in black and white and the remainder in color.

Marilyn and Joe

1954   The most celebrated female film star of her time, Marilyn Monroe married the famous American baseball player Joe DiMaggio in 1954. To generate publicity for her upcoming film *The Seven Year Itch*, a scene was filmed in which Monroe is standing on a subway grate, the air lifting up her white dress. The famous photo of the scene made international front pages and incensed DiMaggio. After returning to Hollywood in October, Monroe filed for divorce. They had been married nine months. Despite the divorce, on Monroe's death, DiMaggio placed a twenty-year order for half a dozen roses to be placed on Monroe's grave three times a week.

Miss America

1954   The Miss America pageant was first televised nationally in 1954. The event was broadcast live from the Boardwalk Hall in Atlantic City. Hosted by Bob Russell (in his last time in that role after many years), Lee Meriwether won the crown.

The $64,000 Question

1955   The American game show ran from 1955 to 1958, where contestants answered general-knowledge questions, earning money for each correct answer, with a top prize of $64,000 for the final question. The popularity of the show led to the expression that is still used to this day.

Rebel Without a Cause

1955   James Dean's most celebrated film, *Rebel Without a Cause*, was released, starring Dean as the troubled teenager Jim Stark. Dean died in a car crash in California that same year while traveling to a sports car racing competition. He was just twenty-four years old and became the first actor to receive a posthumous Academy Award nomination (as Best Actor in *East of Eden*) and the only actor to receive two posthumous nominations (the other film was *Giant*).

The Golden Age of Television

1959   The 1950s are commonly known as the "Golden Age of Television." In 1950, around four million (or 9 percent) of Americans owned television sets. By the end of the decade, that number had increased to 44 million (or 86 percent). Owing to the popularity of television, movie attendance and radio listenership declined considerably.

Bigger than *Ben-Hur*

1959   The epic film starring Charlton Heston earned eleven Academy Awards, a record that it held until the film *Titanic* in 1998. *Ben-Hur* had a budget of over $15 million, the largest of any film produced by that time, and over 200 camels, 2,500 horses, and 10,000 extras were used. It was the second-highest-grossing film in history at the time, after *Gone with the Wind*. *Ben-Hur* was actually a remake of a 1925 silent film, and it was adapted from Lew Wallace's 1880 novel *Ben-Hur: A Tale of the Christ*.

Rawhide

1959   This American Western television series began in 1959 and ran for eight seasons and a total of 217 episodes. It starred a young

Clint Eastwood, and his success in the series led him to international fame.

IT'S JUST BUSINESS

Put It on Credit

1950   The first universal credit card that could be used at a number of establishments was introduced by Diners Club in 1950. It was created by businessman Frank McNamara after he suffered the embarrassment of not having enough money to pay for dinner one time. This ushered in America's love of the credit card. The American Express card didn't follow until 1958.

The Bar Code

1951   A machine-readable method of representing data on products, the first bar code was invented by Norman Joseph Woodland and Bernard Silver in the United States in 1951. The invention was based on Morse code, but it wasn't until the 1970s that bar codes became commercially successful and used in supermarkets.

Mr. Potato Head

1952   This popular toy was first distributed by Hasbro in 1952. In April of that year, it became the first-ever toy advertised on television. The original toy cost ninety-eight cents.

No-Cal

1952   The first diet soda was developed in 1952 by industry pioneer Hyman Kirsch. While many believe the first brand was Tab, it was actually called "No-Cal." Originally developed for diabetic hospital patients, using calcium cyclamate as a sugar replacement, by 1953 it was marketed to the public as a drink to help keep weight under control.

Disneyland

1955   The Disneyland amusement park opened in Anaheim, California, and is the only park designed and built under the supervision of Walt Disney himself. More people have visited Disneyland than any other theme park in the world. Born in 1901, Walt Disney holds the record for the most Academy Awards earned and nominations, having won twenty-two Oscars with fifty-nine nominations. He met with fame when he developed the character Mickey Mouse, and it was Disney himself who provided Mickey's voice until 1947.

Let's Go Shopping

1956   The Southdale Center in Edina, Minnesota, opened in 1956 and was the first fully enclosed, climate-controlled shopping mall in the United States.

NASA Is Born

1958   NASA was established by President Eisenhower when he signed the National Aeronautics and Space Act. It began with an annual budget of $100 million. In that same year, the Space Task Group was formed to manage the spaceflight programs, fueled by the pressure of the Cold War and the resultant competition between the United States and the Soviet Union.

Hula-Hoops

1958   The Hula-Hoop craze swept America in the late 1950s. The product was designed by Arthur K. "Spud" Melin and Richard Knerr and was an instant success, selling 25 million in the first four months and more than one hundred million in two years. It is said that Joan Anderson brought a bamboo exercise hoop back from Australia in 1957 and came up with the name at a dinner party. She showed it to her husband, who took it to Melin.

I'm a Barbie Girl...

1959   Launched in 1959 by the American toy company Mattel, Inc., more than a billion Barbie dolls have been sold, making it the company's most profitable toy. The American businesswoman Ruth Handler is credited with creating the doll, and it is thought that she used a German doll called "Bild Lilli" as her inspiration.

The Rich List

1959   The richest man in the world in the 1950s was J. Paul Getty. He made his wealth by investing in oil, and at the time of his death was worth more than $6 billion. He was, however, notably frugal, and negotiated the ransom sum when his grandson was kidnapped in 1973. He was even said to have a pay phone in his house so visitors were unable to make free phone calls.

IN INFAMY

Ten Most Wanted

1950   The brainchild of J. Edgar Hoover, the FBI started the Ten Most Wanted Fugitives list in March of 1950. The first person added to the list was Thomas J. Holden, a notorious robber at the time. As of March 2022, 526 fugitives had made it onto the list, only ten of them women. Of all the people who have made the list, 491 have been either captured or located.

Chinchaga Fire

1950   Also known as "Fire 19," this forest fire burned in Alberta and British Columbia for over four months, burning a size of over four million acres and making it the largest fire in the history of North America. The smoke from the fire resulted in blue-shaded suns and moons across the United States and Europe.

Assassination Attempt

1950   An attempt was made on Harry S. Truman's life by two Puerto Rican nationalists. While the president was not hurt, two Secret Service agents were killed, as was one of the would-be assassins. The other was sentenced to death, but the president commuted his sentence to life in prison.

Earthquake

1950   The ninth largest earthquake of the twentieth century hit parts of Assam and Tibet in August of 1950. It had a magnitude of 8.6. The quake and the resulting floods killed 1,526 people and left over five million without shelter.

Children of Thalidomide

1956   Thalidomide was a drug marketed as a sedative and treatment for morning sickness in the 1950s, but it caused babies to be born with disabilities. The first thalidomide-affected baby was born in Germany on Christmas Day of 1956.

Midair Disaster

1956   Two aircraft, one from United Airlines and one from Trans World Airlines, collided above the Grand Canyon, killing all 128 people on board.

Hurricane Audrey

1957   Hurricane Audrey hit Cameron, Louisiana, killing over four hundred people.

THE WEIRD AND THE WONDERFUL

Telephone Booth Stuffing

1959   The craze of seeing how many people could stuff into a telephone booth swept America after a group of twenty-five students in Durban, South Africa, achieved the feat. Students around America took up the challenge, and a group of twenty-two at St. Mary's College managed to squeeze into a booth in 1959 in Moraga, California.

Conical Bras

1959   Marilyn Monroe and Jayne Mansfield were largely responsible for this strange new trend in bra styles, which continued with Madonna many years later.

Fuzzy Dice

1959   Fuzzy dice were said to originate during World War II when fighter pilots hung them in their cockpits for good luck. But by the late 1950s, they were hung from the rear-view mirrors of American cars, and the fad soon became entrenched, existing to this day.

POP QUIZ HOT SHOT

(HINT: YOU WON'T FIND THE ANSWERS ABOVE)

1. Which European country had a revolution in 1956?

2. Which African country set up concentration camps in the 1950s?

3. Which city was built during the 1950s to become the capital of its country?

4. What important medical invention occurred in the decade?

5. What Frankie Laine hit reached number one in 1950?

6. Name one animated film produced by Walt Disney in the 1950s.

7. Which American artist, known for pop art, rose to fame in the 1950s?

8. In what 1951 film did Humphrey Bogart win the Academy Award for Best Actor?

9. Which famous American boxer was born in May of 1956?

10. What now-common kitchen appliance was first manufactured in 1955?

1. Hungary **2.** Kenya **3.** Brasília **4.** ultrasound for the heart **5.** "Mule Train" **6.** Alice in Wonderland, Cinderella, Peter Pan, Lady and the Tramp, Sleeping Beauty **7.** Andy Warhol **8.** The African Queen **9.** Sugar Ray Leonard **10.** microwave oven

1960s

THE SWINGING SIXTIES

Also known as the "Cultural Decade," the 1960s are often referred to as the "Swinging Sixties" because of the revolution that occurred in terms of civil rights, music, dress, drugs, and sexuality. In addition to heightened Cold War tensions between the United States and the Soviet Union, the decade is remarkable in terms of the number of historically significant events that occurred. The first man on the moon; the assassination of John F. Kennedy and his brother, as well as Martin Luther King Jr.; and the Woodstock festival, just to name a few. It also saw the United States enter the Vietnam War and the public's resultant conflict about the continued war effort.

HIGH SOCIETY

Mop Tops and Miniskirts

1960 The Beatles had an extensive influence on the hairstyles of the 1960s, with their trademark mop-top cut being sported by many young men. The British fashion designer Mary Quant popularized the miniskirt and hot pants in the decade, while the beehive hairstyle became popular among women. The bikini continued the popularity it had gained during the previous decade, while the hippie movement influenced fashion, with tie-dye and paisley shirts, as well as bell-bottom jeans.

Growth

1965   The 1960s saw the world economy prosper, with the expansion of the middle classes. While the decade began with a recession, by the middle of the sixties, America's unemployment was down to 3.7 percent and inflation was below 2 percent. But with the Nixon administration, by the end of the decade unemployment was at 3.5 percent and inflation was at 6.2 percent.

Flower Power

1965   The second half of the decade witnessed a social revolution, as the younger generations rebelled against mainstream conservatism and materialism. Known as hippies, the youth of the time were in favor of liberalism, fighting for the rights of minorities and women, demanding sexual freedom, and rebelling against conformity. With this revolution came widespread drug use, such as LSD and marijuana. "Flower power" became a slogan used as a symbol of passive, as opposed to violent, resistance, and its proponents often wore vibrantly colored clothing and had long, flowing hair. The term is said to have been coined by the American Beat poet Allen Ginsberg, and it became a symbol of the anti-war movement.

Women's Liberation

1963   The women's liberation movement campaigned for women to have equal status in society and to have the right to do the same jobs as men and to earn the same pay. This was largely triggered by the 1963 release of the book *The Feminine Mystique* by writer Betty Friedan. Feminists marched and protested, and by 1968, the term "women's liberation" had become commonplace.

Woodstock

1969   Arguably the most famous music festival in history, this three-day event on a dairy farm in upstate New York featured some of the world's biggest bands and promoted the hippie youth movement based on love and peace. An audience of more than 400,000 saw thirty-two acts, including Jimi Hendrix, the Who, Creedence Clearwater Revival, the Band, and Jefferson Airplane. The festival is widely regarded as a defining event for the counterculture movement.

Generation X

1965   The 1960s saw the world's population growth increase with "Generation X." The world population increased 22 percent in the decade, compared with 20 percent in the 1950s. By the end of the decade, there were just over 203 million Americans, up over 13 percent from the start of the decade.

Decline in Farming

1965   America's society continued to move toward an industrial one during the 1960s, as the traditional farming life was further eroded because millions of people relocated to the cities. Nearly a million small farms disappeared in the decade, with the average farm size increasing significantly.

Crime on the Rise

1969   The levels of crime in the United States increased markedly during the decade, never to return to the levels of the pre-1960s. Violent crime almost doubled by the close of the decade.

The Law of Averages

1969   The average family income rose from $5,600 in 1960 to $9,400 in 1969, while the average price of a gallon of gas rose from thirty-one cents in 1960 to thirty-four cents in 1969. The minimum wage went to one dollar an hour in 1967. By February 1969, it was at $1.30 an hour.

IT'S A POLITICAL THING

Bay of Pigs

1961   At the height of the Cold War, and covertly managed by the American government, the Bay of Pigs invasion was a failed landing operation by Cuban exiles who opposed Fidel Castro's regime. Trained in Guatemala, over 1,400 paramilitaries landed in the Bay of Pigs. As knowledge of the invasion became widespread, President Kennedy withheld further air support, and the invading force was defeated by the Cubans within three days. Universally regarded as a significant foreign policy failure, the incident widened the gulf between the United States and Cuba, solidified Castro's position as leader of the nation, and brought Cuba and the Soviet Union closer together.

The Berlin Wall

1961   As people in droves left communist East Berlin for the democracy and freedom of the West, the economy of the East declined dramatically. To help stop this, the East Germans built a heavily guarded wall that prevented anyone from leaving. The wall became a symbol of communism and the oppression it stood for.

Independence for Algeria

1962   After being engaged in a war with France since 1954, the French president, Charles de Gaulle, granted Algeria its independence.

Cuban Missile Crisis

1962   Following the use of spy planes to discover that the Soviet Union was installing nuclear weapons in Cuba, President Kennedy demanded that Soviet leader Nikita Khrushchev remove them. This incident almost turned the Cold War into an active war, which may well have become World War III. Following an American naval blockade of Cuba, the Soviets backed down and removed their missiles in exchange for the United States removing its missiles from Turkey.

I Have a Dream

1963   In August of 1963, Martin Luther King Jr. gave his famous speech at a civil rights rally in Washington, DC. It was the largest march of the Civil Rights Movement, with more than 250,000 people descending on the capital demanding the government take action to end racial discrimination. With the crowd in front of the Lincoln Memorial, Dr. King said "I have a dream that one day this nation will rise up and live out the true meaning of its creed... that all men are created equal." The Civil Rights Act was passed the next year. This banned employers from hiring on the basis of color, religion, or national origin. The 1965 Voting Rights Act then prevented states from having requirements designed to stop Black people from voting, then the 1968 Fair Housing Act provided for equality when selling or renting property.

African Unity

1963   After a number of African nations broke free from colonial rule, in 1963 thirty-two African states formed the Organization of African Unity in an attempt to further their economic and political interests. Between 1960 and 1968, thirty-two African countries gained their independence, although many were left unstable, resulting in dictatorships and civil war.

Mandela Jailed

1964   Nelson Mandela was one of the leaders of the African National Congress, a body set up to fight for the rights of Black South Africans. As part of his work, Mandela campaigned against the apartheid regime and was arrested and sent to jail.

Vietnam

1965   In support of South Vietnam and in an attempt to prevent the "domino effect," a theory that if one country fell to communism, others would soon follow, the United States entered the Vietnam conflict that had been going on since the late 1950s. By the end of 1966, more than half a million American troops were sent to the conflict by the Johnson administration. Much of the resistance against American soldiers was provided by the Viet Cong, a group of South Vietnamese communist rebels who fought using guerilla warfare. The Vietnam War was the first in which Americans back home could follow footage on television. Shocked by the violence they were seeing, public anti-war sentiment grew.

Revolution in China

1966   The chairman of the Communist Party of China, Mao Zedong, unveiled the Cultural Revolution in 1966. The aim of the movement was to remove capitalist sympathizers from positions of power in the country. The revolution lasted until 1969, and by that time, hundreds of thousands of people had been killed.

The Troubles in Ireland

1968   The 1960s saw the start of the Northern Ireland conflict, based primarily on the political status of the region. The unionists, or loyalists, wanted Northern Ireland to remain part of the United Kingdom, while the Irish nationalists, or republicans, wanted the area to join Ireland and be united. Years of bloodshed ensued, the violence often spilling into England.

France Strikes

1968   Student riots erupted in Paris in 1968 over the government's education policy. This led to more than ten million workers going on strike and demanding higher wages. The protests continued until the government stood down and elections were called.

Invasion of Czechoslovakia

1968   In an attempt to give the people more freedom, the new leader of the communist country, Alexander Dubček, initiated a program of reform called "Prague Spring." This began in January 1968, but the reforms ended in August when the Soviet Union invaded the country to suppress them.

The Stonewall Riots

1969   Occurring in June 1969 in New York City, the Stonewall Riots were a series of violent demonstrations by members of the gay community in response to a raid by the police of the Stonewall Inn in Greenwich Village. The riots are thought to be the first time the gay community had fought for their rights, and they became a defining event that began the gay rights movement in the United States.

Gaddafi to Power

1969　On September 1, 1969, Muammar al-Gaddafi, a young army officer, seized power in Libya, overthrowing the monarchy while the king was out of the country.

A SCIENTIFIC WORLD

Inventions

1960　The 1960s bore witness to a number of technological inventions, including BASIC, an early computer language, in 1964; the halogen lamp in 1960; the Kevlar vest in 1965; the first compact disc in 1965; the computer mouse in 1967; the first handheld calculator in 1967; and the RAM chip in 1968. The first functioning laser was invented in 1960 by Theodore Maiman, while the first electronic cigarette, called the "Smokeless," was created by Herbert A. Gilbert in 1963.

Bombs Away

1960　France detonated its first atomic bomb in 1960 and had a hydrogen bomb by 1968. China followed in 1964, detonating its first atomic bomb. It had a hydrogen bomb by 1967.

The Pill

1960　The FDA (US Food and Drug Administration) approved the first female birth-control contraceptive, known as "the pill," which was released in 1960.

Unimate

1961   Unimate was the first industrial robot. It worked on a General Motors assembly line in New Jersey in 1961, where it extracted hot metal parts from a casting machine.

First Man in Space

1961   The Soviet pilot Yuri Gagarin became the first man to travel into space in the rocket *Vostok 1*. He took just under two hours to orbit Earth, and from then on he was a household name.

Telstar 1

1962   Just one year after Yuri Gagarin went into space, the United States launched the first communications satellite, Telstar 1. It was used to relay telephone, telegraph, and television signals to Earth. But the project was a failure, and technical faults ended the satellite's tenure in less than a year.

Touch-Tone Dialing

1963   The first touch-tone telephone was introduced in the United States in 1963.

The Big Bang

1964   Cosmic microwave background, an electromagnetic radiation that is said to be a remnant from an early stage of the universe, was discovered in 1964, leading scientists to posit the "big bang" as the most likely theory of the universe's beginnings.

The Space Race Goes On

1965   After the first satellite, Sputnik, in 1957, then the first man in space in 1961, the Soviet Union continued its dominance in 1965 when their cosmonaut Alexei Leonov became the first man to step outside a spacecraft and do a "space walk." But the Soviet dominance of the distant skies would soon be over.

Heart Transplant

1967   The world's first heart-transplant operation was carried out by Professor Christiaan Barnard, a cardiac surgeon in South Africa, in 1967. The patient was Louis Washkansky, who survived the operation but died from pneumonia eighteen days later.

One Small Step

1969   On July 20, 1969, United States' astronauts Neil Armstrong and Buzz Aldrin became the first men to set foot on the moon after successfully landing the spacecraft *Apollo 11*. "That's one small step for man, one giant leap for mankind," Neil Armstrong said as millions of people around the world tuned in to their televisions for the historic event.

Concorde

1969   March of 1969 saw the first flight of Concorde, the supersonic aircraft. It was capable of traveling more than twice the speed of sound, or more than 1,350 miles per hour.

MUSIC AND THE ARTS

The End of Rock (for Now)

1960   The rock 'n' roll dominance of the 1950s came to an end in the early sixties as Elvis Presley joined the army. At the same time, other rock acts fell off the charts.

The Rat Pack

1960   Led by Frank Sinatra and also featuring Dean Martin, Sammy Davis Jr., Peter Lawford, and Joey Bishop, the Rat Pack was a group of famous entertainers who appeared together on stage in Las Vegas and in films in the 1960s, including *Oceans 11*.

Ernest Hemingway Dies

1961   Famous American writer Ernest Hemingway died by a self-inflicted gunshot wound to the head on July 2, 1961. With increasing paranoia and a decline in his mental health, Hemingway put a shotgun in his mouth and pulled the trigger at his home in Ketchum, Idaho. He was sixty-one. Hemingway had cheated death a number of times in his life, including being hit by an Austrian mortar shell on the Italian front in World War I, being shot while shark fishing in 1935, and surviving two plane crashes in two days while in Africa in 1954.

Beatlemania

1962   The Beatles released their first single, "Love Me Do," in 1962. The group traveled to America, and after they appeared on *The Ed Sullivan Show* in 1964, their sales skyrocketed and the nation became obsessed. Other British groups, such as the Kinks and the Rolling Stones, soon followed. With estimated worldwide sales of over 600 million, the Beatles are the best-selling musical act of all time.

Bob Dylan

1963   Born Robert Zimmerman, Bob Dylan's American folk music of the 1960s defined the counterculture of the time, with songs such as "Blowin' in the Wind" and "The Times They Are A-Changin'" becoming anthems for the anti-war and civil rights movements. Often regarded as one of the greatest songwriters of all time, Dylan has sold more than 125 million records.

Surf Rock

1963 At the same time as Bob Dylan's songs were gaining in popularity, so too was the surf rock that emerged, led principally by the California band the Beach Boys, comprising the three Wilson brothers: Brian, Dennis, and Carl, and a cousin and a friend.

The Man in Black

1968 After performing concerts at prisons in the 1950s, Johnny Cash recorded the albums *Johnny Cash at Folsom Prison* and *Johnny Cash at San Quentin* in 1968 and 1969 respectively. The albums were a huge success, both going to the top of the country and pop charts.

The King Is Back

1968 After spending most of the 1960s making films, Elvis Presley famously returned to performing music with the '68 *Comeback Special*, which was broadcast on NBC in December of that year. The performance was the most watched show of the season and relaunched "the King's" singing career.

Andy Warhol Shot

1968 The American pop artist Andy Warhol was shot and almost killed by radical feminist Valerie Solanas.

Literature Booms

1969 The 1960s saw the publication of many books that would come to enduring fame, including *To Kill a Mockingbird* (1960), *Catch-22* (1961), *One Flew Over the Cuckoo's Nest* (1962), *A Clockwork Orange* (1962), *An American Dream* (1965), *The Tiger Who Came to Tea* (1968), *The Godfather* (1969), and *The Very Hungry Caterpillar* (1969).

Jack Kerouac Dies

1969   Jack Kerouac, the American novelist and pioneer of the Beat generation, died in October of 1969. He suffered an abdominal hemorrhage caused by a lifetime of heavy drinking.

A SPORTING LIFE

Olympics

1960   The decade began with the Summer Olympic Games held in Rome, Italy. The Soviet Union topped the medal table, followed by the United States. Next were the 1964 Olympic Games in Tokyo, in which South Africa was banned due to its policies of apartheid in sports. This time, the United States won, followed by the Soviet Union. The final Olympic Games of the decade were held in Mexico City, with the United States again winning, followed by the Soviet Union. One of the most famous photographs of the decade came from the Mexico games, when African American sprinters Tommie Smith and John Carlos, the gold and bronze medalists in the 200 meters, stood on the podium during the medal ceremony wearing human rights badges and black socks without shoes while each lowered their heads and raised a black-gloved fist. This show of support for the Black freedom movement created much controversy and led to their expulsion from the games.

I Am the Greatest!

1964   After winning gold in the light-heavyweight boxing division of the 1960 Rome Olympic Games, Muhammad Ali (born Cassius Clay) won the world heavyweight championship in February of 1964 at the age of twenty-two. He defeated the reigning champion, Sonny Liston, in one of the biggest upsets in boxing history. In that same year,

Clay became Ali, renouncing what he called his "slave name." But in 1966 he refused to be drafted into the military and was stripped of his title.

Baseball's Expansion

1969 Major League Baseball expanded considerably during the 1960s. The Los Angeles Angels were formed in 1961, as were the Washington Senators. Then, in 1962, the New York Mets and the Houston Colt .45s were sanctioned. In 1969, after only eight years, the New York Mets won the World Series.

The Celtics

1969 The Boston Celtics dominated the NBA during the 1960s. With players like Bob Cousy, Bill Russell, and John Havlicek, they won nine of the titles.

Green Bay

1969 The Green Bay Packers won five championships during the decade, while the New York Giants were runners up three times.

THE BIG (AND SMALL) SCREEN

The Flintstones

1960 This American animated sitcom was broadcast on the ABC network from 1960 to 1966. It was produced by Hanna-Barbera Productions and was the first animated series to be shown in prime time. *The Flintstones* was the most successful animated television series for thirty years. Over forty million people saw each episode.

Marilyn Dies

1962   Hollywood starlet Marilyn Monroe died in 1962 at the age of just thirty-six from an overdose of sleeping pills. While her death was ruled a probable suicide, much speculation and many conspiracy theories still surround the circumstances, especially whether she was murdered because of her involvement with President John F. Kennedy and his brother Bobby, the United States attorney general at the time.

The Man with No Name

1964   Sergio Leone's spaghetti Western trilogy began in 1964 with *A Fistful of Dollars*, followed by *For a Few Dollars More* (1965), and *The Good, The Bad and The Ugly* (1966). All three films starred Clint Eastwood as the laconic Western gunslinger with no name. The films were a success and made Eastwood an instant household name, propelling his film career.

The Sound of Music

1965   While *Mary Poppins* (1964) and *My Fair Lady* (1964) were huge box office successes, it was *The Sound of Music* in 1965, produced by 20th Century Fox, that was the highest-grossing film of the decade.

ZAP! POW!

1966   Based on the DC comic book character, 120 episodes of *Batman* were aired by ABC between 1966 and 1968. The show starred Adam West as the title character, with Burt Ward as his cape-crusading sidekick.

Walt Disney Dies

1966   The famous filmmaker died in December of 1966 at the age of sixty-four. A heavy smoker, he died of circulatory collapse associated with the lung cancer he had contracted.

Easy Rider

1969   The independent film *Easy Rider*, starring Peter Fonda, Dennis Hopper, and Jack Nicholson, quickly became a counterculture film with its depiction of drug use and a free-living lifestyle. It received two Academy Award nominations: Best Original Screenplay and Best Supporting Actor for Jack Nicholson.

The Brady Bunch

1969   This American sitcom was broadcast on ABC from 1969 to 1974. While it was not a popular or critical success at the time, once in syndication, the show developed a large fan base.

IT'S JUST BUSINESS

Wall Street

1962   The year 1962 was the worst for the Dow Jones Industrial Average since the Great Depression in 1931. In the first six months of that year, it declined by 27 percent. But it quickly recovered, and by January 1966, it rose to over 1,000. And in the period from 1962 to 1968, the market increased even more than it had during the boom of the 1920s. During the 1960s, around thirty million Americans owned stocks.

The Chain Store

1962   The 1960s saw the beginning of the discount chain store, with Kmart the first discount retailer. Its first store opened in 1962 in Garden City, Michigan. Walmart and Target also opened for business in that year. The opening of these large chains changed the shopping habits of American consumers, who had previously bought products from independent mom-and-pop stores.

Nike

1964   The American multinational corporation that manufactures sportswear, Nike was founded in 1964. It began as Blue Ribbon Sports, set up by Bill Bowerman and Phil Knight, changing its name to Nike, Inc. in 1971. As of 2020, the company employed almost 77,000 people worldwide and had revenues of over $37 billion.

High-Speed Rail

1964   Shinkansen, known as the bullet train, was the world's first high-speed rail service, which began operating in Japan in 1964.

Cars, Cars, Cars

1965   The car industry developed dramatically in the United States in the 1960s. The stylish cars of the 1950s were replaced with more boxy designs. The first hatchback, the Renault 16, was introduced in 1965. Japanese cars also began to infiltrate the American market by the middle of the decade.

Automated Banking

1967   The first automatic teller machine (ATM) was opened in London by Barclays Bank.

The Gap

1969   This famous clothing store was founded in 1969 by Donald Fisher and Doris F. Fisher. The first Gap opened on Ocean Avenue in the Ingleside neighborhood of San Francisco in that same year, and the only merchandise it stocked were Levi's jeans. There are now around three thousand stores worldwide.

A Tobacco Change

1969   Threatened by increasing medical research that indicated smoking was a serious health hazard, large tobacco companies began diversifying. American Tobacco bought companies such as Master Lock, Sunshine Biscuits, Jim Beam, and Franklin Life Insurance. Then, in 1969, its name was changed to American Brands. Philip Morris bought the Seven-Up Company and Miller Brewing.

IN INFAMY

Valdivia Earthquake

1960   Also known as the "great Chilean earthquake," it had a Richter rating of 9.5 and is the most powerful earthquake ever recorded. It caused tsunamis that hit the Chilean coast, and the primary tsunami went across the Pacific Ocean, destroying Hilo, Hawaii.

Midair Disaster

1960   Two aircraft, one from United Airlines and one from Trans World Airlines, collided over New York City, killing all 128 people on board and six people on the ground.

Escape from Alcatraz

1962   The Alcatraz Federal Penitentiary on Alcatraz Island in San Francisco Bay operated between 1934 and 1963. In that time, there were fourteen escapes attempted by thirty-four prisoners. But it was the escape by Frank Morris and brothers John and Clarence Anglin, in June of 1962, that is the most famous. After using papier-mâché heads to make it seem like they were asleep in bed, they broke out of the main prison through an unused utility door and set off into the bay on a makeshift inflatable raft. After many investigations, the FBI finally concluded that the men had likely drowned in the bay, although their bodies were never found.

President Kennedy Assassinated

1963   In one of the most famous incidents in history, President John F. Kennedy was assassinated in November 1963 while a passenger in an open-top car in Dallas. The assassin was named as Lee Harvey Oswald. Oswald was arrested, but subsequently killed by Jack Ruby on live television in the basement of the Dallas Police Department while being transferred to jail before standing trial. Kennedy's assassination has been the subject of numerous conspiracy theories, including the belief by many that a single bullet could not have been possible. This became known as the "magic-bullet theory." The notoriety of the assassination and the resultant shock of the nation led to the common question: "Where were you when you heard the news that President Kennedy had been shot?"

Malcolm X

1965   The prominent Muslim minister and human rights activist was assassinated on February 21 in the Audubon Ballroom in the Washington Heights neighborhood of New York City. Controversy still exists as to who was responsible for his death.

Che Guevara Killed

1967   Ernesto "Che" Guevara was killed by US troops in Bolivia in 1967. A leading figure in the Cuban Revolution, Guevara had left Cuba to start communist uprisings in other countries. The image of his face became a popular symbol of revolution and is still widely recognizable today.

Martin Luther King Jr. Assassinated

1968   Martin Luther King Jr. was assassinated on April 4, 1968, by James Earl Ray, a lone gunman opposed to the Civil Rights Movement. Dr. King was in Memphis at the time, supporting a strike by Black workers. The assassination triggered race riots across the country. But by the time of his death, and largely due to his efforts, racial segregation had legally ended in America.

Robert Kennedy Killed

1968   In June of 1968, Robert Kennedy, the younger brother of the former president, was killed while campaigning to become the Democratic nominee for president. He had just won the California primary. His killer was Sirhan Sirhan, a Palestinian who had objected to Kennedy's support of Israel in the Six-Day War of 1967.

Manson Murders

1969   Led by Charles Manson, the Manson family was a California-based cult infamous for a series of nine murders in July and August of 1969, including that of actress Sharon Tate. Manson himself was convicted of first-degree murder and conspiracy to commit murder.

THE WEIRD AND THE WONDERFUL

Breast Implants

1961   The silicone-gel breast implant was invented in 1961 by American plastic surgeons Frank Gerow and Thomas Cronin. Manufactured by Dow Corning Corporation, the first augmentation was performed in 1962.

Smiley Face

1963   While working for an advertising agency in Massachusetts in 1963, graphic designer Harvey Ross Ball came up with the smiley face and was paid forty-five dollars for it. The drawing was commissioned by State Mutual Life Assurance Company to create an image to help boost staff morale.

Lava Lamps

1963   Lava lamps were invented by British entrepreneur Edward Craven Walker. By the late 1960s, the lamps had become extremely popular, often favored by the hippie movement.

Tie-Dye

1969   Also fueled by the hippie movement, the fad of tie-dying T-shirts became hugely popular in the late 1960s, particularly in California. The process involved twisting or crumpling a shirt before applying the dye, so that the dye didn't fully cover the garment but would leave it with psychedelic patterns.

1. Which European colonial war began in 1961?

2. In what year did the National Farmers Organization withhold milk supplies for fifteen days to help stabilize prices?

3. Which two American political leaders were involved in the first presidential debates held on live television?

4. Whom did Richard Nixon defeat to become president in 1968?

5. What significance did Valentina Tereshkova have in the space race in 1963?

6. Name one of two songs that reached number one in the country charts for Tammy Wynette in 1963.

7. In what 1967 film did a Simon and Garfunkel hit song feature?

8. Who starred in the main role in the American television series *The Fugitive* that ran from 1963 to 1967?

9. The bird's nest and the chignon were both types of what in the 1960s?

10. To what now well-known number was the first call placed in 1968?

1. Portuguese **2.** 1967 **3.** Richard Nixon and John F. Kennedy **4.** Vice President Hubert H. Humphrey **5.** the first woman in space **6.** "D-I-V-O-R-C-E" and "Stand By Your Man" **7.** *The Graduate* ("Mrs. Robinson" was the song) **8.** David Janssen **9.** hairstyles **10.** 911

1970s

THE ME DECADE

Also known as a decade of change, it was the American writer Tom Wolfe who dubbed the 1970s "the Me Decade." He was describing the change in concerns of many people from issues of political and social injustice in the 1960s to a more personal focus of individual well-being. This may be attributed to the decline of the economy in the 1970s, primarily due to an oil crisis, which caused many Americans to focus their attention on their own economic problems, rather than on the issues of society. But the decade was no less tumultuous on a political front, with a multitude of wars and civil unrest occurring, as well as one of the biggest scandals in American history—Watergate. The decade also saw great developments in science as well as advancements in technology, with personal computers and other electronic accessories hitting the mass market. And as women began to play a greater role in society, it was all change for Generation X.

Women in the Workforce

1970   The 1970s witnessed a greater number of women enter the workforce, both in the United States and in other industrialized societies, as feminism gained in popularity. Despite this, the men of the US remained in the role of primary family breadwinner. Women also began to lead countries, most notably Margaret Thatcher in Britain.

Bell-Bottoms and Farrah Hair

1970   Starting with the hippie movement of the 1960s, bell-bottoms, or flares, became hugely popular in the 1970s, as did hot pants for women. So did the "Farrah-do," the long, feathery hairstyle made famous by American actress and fashion model Farrah Fawcett. Many men sported sideburns, beards, and mustaches. Turtleneck shirts were also commonly worn, although suits came into fashion in the latter part of the decade, influenced by the hugely popular film *Saturday Night Fever*. And throughout 1970s homes, shag carpeting was all the rage.

Earth Day

1970   Environmentalism began to gain widespread support in the 1970s after the United States celebrated its first Earth Day at the start of the decade. Ten thousand schools and two thousand universities and colleges participated in the event, which became an annual event held on April 22.

Right to Vote

1971   In 1971, the US Congress passed the Twenty-Sixth Amendment to the Constitution and lowered the voting age from twenty-one to eighteen years. The major force behind the reduction was that men were being drafted to fight in Vietnam before they were even able to vote.

Reduced Growth

1979   The 1970s saw the lowest rate of growth in world economies since the Great Depression. The oil crises of 1973 and 1979 were major factors in the downturns, during which American manufacturing industries declined and inflation and unemployment rose. By 1979, inflation in the United States topped 13 percent. The combined rate of inflation and unemployment was over 20 percent by the end of the decade, the highest in American history. A "bear market" between January 1973 and December 1974 also affected the world's stock markets. At the same time, led by exports, and with an abundance of cheap labor, the economies of Asia boomed, and Japan overtook the United States as the world's leading manufacturer.

Generation X Continues

1979   The population continued to increase markedly in the United States during the 1970s. At the beginning of the decade, there were just over 203 million Americans, and by the end there were another 23 million.

The Law of Averages

1979   The cost of the average family home rose from around $23,000 in 1970 to almost $70,000 by the end of the decade. The average family income rose from $9,400 in 1970 to $16,530 in 1979. The minimum wage in February 1970 was $1.45 an hour, and by 1979 it was up to $2.90 an hour.

Quebec Problems

1970   In 1970, radical militants of the FLQ kidnapped the Quebec labor minister Pierre Laporte. Laporte was killed in the incident, and martial law was declared in Canada.

Idi Amin

1971   In January 1971, Idi Amin, the commander of the Ugandan Army, overthrew the president to become ruler. While leader, he was responsible for the death of over 100,000 of his countrymen. The Uganda-Tanzania War, which was fought between 1978 and 1979, led to the overthrow of Amin.

Nixon and Mao

1972   After refusing to recognize China's communist regime since 1949, President Richard Nixon became the first United States president to visit China, meeting with Chinese leader Mao Zedong. By 1978, the United States recognized China as a country.

Philippines under Martial Law

1972   In September 1972, Philippine dictator Ferdinand Marcos declared martial law, although he called it "constitutional authoritarianism." His rule was infamous for its corruption and brutality.

Bloody Sunday

1972   The conflict between the Irish nationalists and the unionists made worldwide headlines in 1972 when thirteen unarmed nationalist protestors were shot dead by the British army.

Chilean Coup

1973 In the early 1970s, Chile was a democratic country led by Salvador Allende. But in 1973, the head of the army, General Augusto Pinochet, led a coup that ousted Allende. Pinochet would stand as the Chilean dictator until 1990.

Yom Kippur

1973 Egyptian and Syrian forces launched an attack on Israel on the holiest day of the Jewish year. The United States and other Western countries supported Israel in their successful resistance. As a result, Arab nations cut oil supplies to the West until March 1974, which led to fuel shortages and triggered a global recession.

Invasion of Cyprus

1974 In an attempt to prevent it from becoming part of Greece, Turkey invaded the island of Cyprus.

Vietnam Over

1975 Despite US troops withdrawing from the Vietnam conflict in 1973, fighting between the North and the South continued until 1975, with the unconditional surrender of the South, following the fall of Saigon. Prior to the withdrawal of the United States, anti-war demonstrations were rife in America. A famous protest was held at Kent State University, Ohio, in 1970, and the National Guard was called in. It ended in disaster when four students were shot and killed, and nine others were injured.

Further African Decolonization

1975 Africa continued its decolonization with Mozambique and Angola gaining independence from the Portuguese.

Civil War in Lebanon

1975   Tensions between the Christians and Palestinian refugees led by the Palestinian Liberation Organization came to a head when armed Christians attacked a bus full of Palestinians in Beirut. A fifteen-year civil war ensued.

Pol Pot

1975   Leader of Cambodia's communist party, the Khmer Rouge, Pol Pot overthrew the US-backed government of Lon Nol and tried to return the country to a Marxist rural society. He emptied cities and killed anyone who opposed him. His regime ended when Vietnam invaded in 1979, overthrowing the Khmer Rouge. By that time, Pol Pot had killed an estimated three million people, including many of the country's educated.

Western Sahara War

1975   A war between Morocco and the Sahrawi indigenous Polisario Front began in 1975 after Spain withdrew from the Spanish Sahara. The war lasted until 1991, by which time an estimated 20,000 people had been killed.

Protests in South Africa

1976   Peaceful student protests in Soweto, South Africa, by Black students against the use of the Afrikaans language in schools led to the Soweto uprising, in which 20,000 students took part. The protests were met with severe police brutality, and an estimated 176 people were killed.

Death of Mao Zedong

1976   Mao Zedong died in 1976 at the age of eighty-two. He had been the leader of communist China since the revolution in 1949, but his policies, such as the Great Leap Forward and the Cultural Revolution, led to the death of millions of Chinese.

Coup in Argentina

1976   After the death of President Juan Perón, Perón's widow and vice president, Isabel, became president. Jorge Rafael Videla led a military coup and deposed her in March 1976, becoming the president of Argentina in a dictatorship. Death squads were set up and many students forcibly disappeared.

Year of Three Popes

1978   In August of 1978, Paul VI, who had been pope since 1963, died. He was followed by John Paul, who died thirty-three days later. John Paul II became the third pope of the year, the first non-Italian since 1523.

Russians in Afghanistan

1979   After the communist party of Afghanistan seized power in 1978, the mujahideen, a group of Islamic militants, rebelled against the coup. Soviet troops were sent in to help the communists, which led to ten years of warfare. This act by the Soviets ended the détente policy, which had seen the Cold War tensions between the United States and the Soviet Union lessen throughout the 1970s.

Margaret Thatcher

1979   In 1979, Conservative Party leader Margaret Thatcher become the first female British prime minister. She became known as the "Iron Lady," and her policies and approach divided public opinion.

Oil Crisis

1979   Also known as the 1979 "oil shock" or the "second oil crisis," the 1979 oil crisis occurred as oil production dropped following the Iranian Revolution. The price of crude oil doubled and resulted in fuel shortages and people rushing to gas stations.

Saddam Hussein to Power

1979   Saddam Hussein formally took power and became the fifth president of Iraq in July 1979. A ruthless dictator and perpetrator of many human rights abuses, Hussein is said to have been responsible for the arbitrary killing of around 250,000 people.

A SCIENTIFIC WORLD

Pocket Calculators

1970   The first pocket calculators were produced in Japan in 1970 and were quickly marketed worldwide.

Intel 4004

1971   Released by the Intel Corporation in 1971 and sold for sixty dollars, the Intel 4004 was the first commercially produced microprocessor. The chip design was created by Federico Faggin.

You Have Mail

1971   The first email was transmitted in 1971. The American computer programmer, Ray Tomlinson, set up the program on the ARPANET system, which was the first system able to send messages between users on different hosts. The first email sent was a test by Tomlinson, and it was never saved.

Video Games

1971   *Computer Space*, the first arcade video game, was developed in 1971. It was created by American engineers Ted Dabney and Nolan Bushnell in partnership with Syzygy Engineering. *Computer Space* marked the start of the commercial video game industry.

Floppy Disks

1971   Invented at IBM, the first floppy disks became available in 1971. They had a diameter of eight inches.

Last Man on the Moon

1972   Gene Cernan, an American astronaut on *Apollo 17*, became the last man on the moon on December 13, 1972.

VCRs Available

1972   The first videocassette recording machine (or VCR) hit the market in 1972. Made by Philips, the first model was the N1500.

First MRI

1973   The first MRI image was produced in 1973. Short for magnetic resonance imaging, MRI is a technique used in medicine to scan the body and form images.

Cell Phones

1973   American engineer Martin Cooper invented the first handheld cellular mobile phone in 1973 while working at Motorola. In that same year, he is said to be the first person in history to make a cell phone call. Standing on Sixth Avenue in New York City, he placed the call, which connected him to a base station that Motorola had installed, and into the AT&T landline telephone system. Reporters looked on as he called his main competitor, Joel S. Engel at AT&T, and told him that he was calling from a cell phone. Cooper then led the team that brought the cell phone to the public market in 1983.

Genetic Engineering

1973   The first organisms to be genetically engineered were bacteria. This occurred in 1973, followed by mice in 1974.

Lucy

1974   In 1974, one of mankind's oldest ancestors was uncovered by scientists in Ethiopia. The team was led by American paleoanthropologist Donald Carl Johanson. The team uncovered the fossil remains of an apelike female biped who lived over 3.2 million years ago. The species was named *Australopithecus afarensis*, but the fossil became better known as "Lucy."

IVF First

1978   Louise Brown became the first human to be born following conception via IVF (in vitro fertilization). Said to be one of the most remarkable medical breakthroughs of the twentieth century, she was born in Oldham General Hospital in England by caesarean section and weighed five pounds, twelve ounces.

Smallpox Eradicated

1979   After the last naturally occurring case in 1977, the World Health Organization certified the eradication of smallpox in December of 1979. Before vaccines were developed, the disease had a death rate of around 30 percent and was responsible for the death of around five hundred million people in one hundred years.

Microwave Ovens

1979   Microwave ovens became commonplace household items by the late 1970s.

Voicemail Begins

1979   The first voicemail system was developed by American inventor Gordon Matthews in 1979. He filed a patent for it in that year. Some claim that Stephen Boies of IBM was the first inventor of voicemail in 1973. Either way, it occurred in the seventies.

MUSIC AND THE ARTS

Buy the Ticket, Take the Ride

1971   Famous for his gonzo journalism style, Hunter S. Thompson was an influential writer in the 1970s, best known for his 1971 book *Fear and Loathing in Las Vegas*. He was a keen political commentator and critic of Richard Nixon, and he even ran for sheriff of Pitkin County, Colorado, in 1970, narrowly losing.

Eagles

1971   Formed in Los Angeles in 1971, the Eagles were one of the most popular bands of the 1970s. With hits such as "Hotel California,"

"Take It Easy," and "Desperado," they have sold more than two hundred million records and are the best-selling band in American history. Originally band members for Linda Ronstadt, the Eagles, led by Glenn Frey and Don Henley, went out on their own and released their first album in 1972.

The Twenty-Seven Club

1971   The 1970s saw the deaths of a number of famous musicians, including Bing Crosby in 1977, who sold an estimated fifty million records. But it was the premature deaths of Jimi Hendrix, Janis Joplin, and Jim Morrison in the early seventies, all aged twenty-seven, that shocked the public.

Hot August Night

1972   *Hot August Night* is a live album by American singer Neil Diamond, recorded at the Greek Theatre in Los Angeles and released in 1972. It became one of the biggest-selling albums of all time in Australia and made Diamond a household name. Diamond has now sold over one hundred million records worldwide, making him one of the best-selling artists in history.

The Dark Side of the Moon

1973   The English progressive rock group Pink Floyd had the best-selling album of the decade with *The Dark Side of the Moon*. For 741 weeks it remained on the Billboard 200 albums chart.

Piano Man

1973   Having performed since the sixties, it was the release of Billy Joel's album *Piano Man* in 1973 that made him a household name. He is the fourth best-selling solo artist in United States history and has sold more than 160 million records worldwide.

Stephen King

1974   Horror novelist Stephen King broke through with the publication of his novel *Carrie* in 1974. Dubbed the "King of Horror," he has sold over 350 million books, many of which have been adapted to film or television.

Motown

1975   With artists such as Marvin Gaye, the Jackson 5, and Stevie Wonder, the 1970s saw Motown music increase in popularity.

Disco

1975   By the mid-1970s, disco music had become very popular, with bands such as ABBA, Bee Gees, and Village People. ABBA, the Swedish pop group, became one of the best-selling bands of all time, with an estimated 350 million records sold.

Rock

1975   In response to the disco trend, rock music became more hard core, with acts such as Deep Purple, Jimi Hendrix, and Led Zeppelin.

Punk Rock

1976   Punk rockers brought a new wave of music that exploded onto the scene in the 1970s. With their spiked hair, shouted lyrics, and aggression, bands such as the Sex Pistols, led by Johnny Rotten, caused quite a stir.

Outlaws

1977   Country music gained in popularity in the 1970s, fueled by Waylon Jennings and Willie Nelson, who led the outlaw movement, refusing to follow the established rules of music. Kenny Rogers and Dolly Parton were also very popular, as were George Jones and Tammy Wynette.

The King Is Dead

1977   On August 16, 1977, Elvis Presley, the "king of rock 'n' roll," died of cardiac arrest at Graceland, his home in Memphis, Tennessee. Elvis was grossly overweight at the time and had been using drugs, twice that year overdosing on barbiturates. He was forty-two years old, the same age as his mother when she died. Elvis's funeral was held at Graceland and around 80,000 people lined the route to Forest Hill Cemetery, where he was buried next to his mother. After attempts to steal Elvis's body later that month, both Presley and his mother were moved and reburied at Graceland.

Led Zeppelin and Elton John

1979   The English artists Led Zeppelin and Elton John (born Reginald Dwight) were the most successful acts of the decade, each selling more than three hundred million records.

A SPORTING LIFE

Olympics

1972   In the 1972 Summer Olympic Games in Munich, American swimmer Mark Spitz won a record seven gold medals in the pool, setting seven world records as he did. The Soviet Union won the games, with the United States coming second. But the games were overshadowed by more sinister events. Eleven members of the Israeli Olympic team were taken hostage by Black September, the Palestinian terrorist group. German authorities tried to rescue the hostages, but all of the hostages and most of the terrorists ended up being killed.

Dolphins Go All the Way

1972   While the NFL was dominated in the seventies by the Dallas Cowboys and the Pittsburgh Steelers, 1972 saw the Miami Dolphins go "all the way" and win the Super Bowl undefeated for the season. It was the first time this had been done, and it hasn't been done since.

The Rumble in the Jungle

1974   Heavyweight boxing during the 1970s was dominated by the fierce rivalry between Americans Muhammad Ali, Joe Frazier, and George Foreman. Ali beat the overwhelming favorite George Foreman in "The Rumble in the Jungle" in Zaire, Africa, in 1974, then went on to beat Joe Frazier in the much-publicized "Thrilla in Manila" in 1975. Elsewhere in boxing, Sugar Ray Leonard won his first title in 1979, beating the Puerto Rican fighter Wilfred Benitez in Las Vegas for the WBC welterweight belt.

Nadia

1976   The 1976 Summer Olympic Games in Montreal are most remembered for the fourteen-year-old Romanian gymnast Nadia Comaneci, who scored seven perfect 10s and won three gold medals. She was the first gymnast in history to get a perfect score. The Soviet Union topped the medal count for the Olympic Games, with the United States coming in third, behind East Germany.

Tennis

1979   Professional tennis witnessed some of the greatest rivalries in the history of the sport during the decade, with the likes of Jimmy Connors, John McEnroe, and Bjorn Borg competing. While Australians John Newcombe and Ken Rosewall dominated world tennis early in the decade, the newcomers soon took over. During the 1970s, Borg won both the French Open and Wimbledon titles four times, while Jimmy Connors won the US Open three times, as well as the Australian Open and Wimbledon in 1974 (a year he also won the US Open). Having turned professional in 1978, McEnroe's first Grand Slam title was the US Open in 1979. Meanwhile, the women's game was dominated in the 1970s by Americans Chris Evert, who won nine Grand Slam titles in the decade, and Billie Jean King, who won seven.

The Athletics, the Reds, and the Yankees

1979   These three clubs dominated baseball in the 1970s. The Oakland Athletics won the World Series three consecutive times from 1972 to 1974. The Cincinnati Reds competed for four titles, winning two, and the New York Yankees won the World Series in 1977 and 1978.

Basketball Split

1979   No one team dominated the NBA during the 1970s. Eight different teams won the NBA, with the Boston Celtics the only team managing to do it twice.

THE BIG (AND SMALL) SCREEN

All in the Family

1971   Airing for nine seasons from 1971 to 1979, the American television sitcom *All in the Family* was the most watched show each year from 1971 to 1975.

Adult Entertainment

1972   The seventies saw the explosion of the adult entertainment industry and an increase in adult movie theaters. The 1972 X-rated film *Behind the Green Door* became one of the highest-grossing films of the year.

Bruce Lee Dies

1973   Bruce Lee, the Hong Kong and American martial artist and actor, died in Hong Kong of a cerebral edema at age thirty-two in 1973. He came to fame for his martial arts action films, including *The Big Boss* in 1971 and *Fists of Fury* in 1972.

The Godfather

1974   With Marlon Brando playing the lead role and winning an Academy Award for Best Actor, *The Godfather*, based on the best-selling 1969 novel by Mario Puzo, won Best Picture. *The Godfather Part II* then went on to win Best Picture in 1974.

Happy Days

1976   With 255 episodes airing over eleven seasons, American television sitcom *Happy Days* was the number one show in the United

States in 1976. The character of Fonzie (played by Henry Winkler) became highly merchandised. The show spawned the hit spin-offs *Laverne & Shirley* (which was the most watched show in 1977 and 1978) and *Mork & Mindy*.

Rocky

1976   The famous boxing film series written by and starring Sylvester Stallone launched in 1976 with *Rocky*. It was made on a budget of under $1 million and was the highest-grossing film of the year, earning $225 million. The film made Stallone a star, and there have been eight sequels.

Star Wars

1977   Written and directed by George Lucas, *Star Wars* was the highest-grossing film of the decade, making $775 million and spawning an industry of toys, games, and clothing (not to mention sequels). The next highest-grossing films of the decade were *Jaws*, *Grease*, and *The Exorcist*.

Dallas

1978   The American soap opera *Dallas* premiered in 1978. CBS aired 357 episodes, and this spurred a resurgence of prime-time soap operas in the United States.

Superman

1978   Starring Christopher Reeve, *Superman* was released in 1978 and was the most expensive film ever made at the time, costing $55 million. It took in $300 million at the box office. Marlon Brando played Superman's father, Jor-El, and was paid an unprecedented $3.7 million plus 11.75 percent of profits for less than twenty minutes on screen.

This amounted to around $19 million. Christopher Reeve was paid $250,000.

Female Leads

1979   By the end of the decade, women were starting to play a larger role as the leads in a number of hit programs, including *Charlie's Angels*, *Police Woman*, *The Bionic Woman*, and *Wonder Woman*. Another famous show with a female lead was *The Mary Tyler Moore Show*, which began in 1970.

IT'S JUST BUSINESS

Amtrak Formed

1971   The National Railroad Passenger Corporation, commonly known under its trade name of Amtrak, was founded in 1971 to provide intercity rail services across North America.

Evel Knievel Toy

1972   Based on the American motorcycle stunt performer, the Evel Knievel toy figure was released by the Ideal Toy Company in 1972. It was hugely popular and, with the other Evel Knievel merchandise, sold $125 million worth.

Magnavox Odyssey

1972   The first commercial home video game console was released in the United States in September of 1972. It was designed by German-American Ralph H. Baer at Sanders Associates.

Japanese Cars

1972   The Japanese car industry boomed in the 1970s, and Japanese cars became available throughout the world. The Honda Civic was introduced in 1972, and in 1975, Toyota had overtaken Volkswagen as the best-selling foreign car brand in the United States.

Sears Tower

1973   Completed in 1973, the Sears Tower in Chicago became the world's tallest building, standing at 1,451 feet. Now called the "Willis Tower," it held the title until Dubai's Burj Khalifa was built. Prior to the construction of the Sears Tower, the World Trade Center towers had been the world's tallest buildings since 1972.

Microsoft

1975   Bill Gates founded his computer company in 1975. By 1995 he was the richest man in the world.

Apple

1976   Apple Computer Company was founded in 1976. Under the leadership of cofounder Steve Jobs, Apple 1, the company's first personal computer, was launched in that same year. In time, the company grew to become one of the most valuable and recognizable in the world.

Atari

1977   After the company was established in 1972, Atari launched its home video game console, the Atari 2600, in 1977. It came with two joysticks and a game cartridge for *Combat*.

Space Invaders

1978   Developed by Tomohiro Nishikado, the Japanese video game engineer, *Space Invaders* came out in 1978. Considered one of the most influential games of all time, it was the first fixed shooter game, and it transformed the video game industry into a worldwide phenomenon. It is the highest-grossing video game of all time.

The First Walkman

1979   Sony released its first Walkman in 1979. It was a portable music cassette player and quickly became hugely popular. By the time Sony stopped production in 2010, two hundred million Walkman units had been sold.

IN INFAMY

Palestinian Hijackings

1970   Three passenger aircrafts were hijacked by Palestinian terrorists in 1970. The planes were taken to an airfield in the Jordanian desert, where they were blown up. The forty passengers were taken hostage but were later freed in return for the release of seven Palestinian prisoners from Western jails.

Cyclone in Pakistan

1970   More than half a million people were killed when the deadliest cyclone on record hit East Pakistan. West Pakistan provided very little help, which triggered an outcry for Eastern independence. This was obtained in 1972 with the formation of Bangladesh.

Genocide in Bangladesh

1971   "Operation Searchlight" was the code name for a military operation undertaken by the Pakistan Army against the Bengali nationalists in East Pakistan (now Bangladesh). A war ensued in which an estimated three million people were killed, making it the largest genocide since the Holocaust.

Capital Punishment

1972   Crime in the United States increased dramatically during the decade, with large urban areas, most notably New York City, the worst affected. In 1972, the US Supreme Court ruled that capital punishment was unconstitutional, but the court reversed the ruling in 1976.

Super Outbreak

1974   In April of 1974, the "Super Outbreak" occurred in the United States. At the time, it was the largest tornado outbreak on record for a twenty-four hour period, with 148 tornadoes in thirteen states. The Super Outbreak killed 330 people.

Watergate

1974   In one of the biggest scandals in American history, President Nixon resigned after it was found that he was involved in the bugging of the Democratic Party's headquarters in the Watergate building in Washington, DC. Nixon's involvement had been proven by an investigation undertaken by the *Washington Post* newspaper. In what became one of the most famous photographs of the decade, Nixon displayed the "V for victory" sign with both arms raised as he boarded a helicopter to depart the White House for the final time.

Emperor of Ethiopia Assassinated

1975   Haile Selassie, the emperor of Ethiopia since 1930, was overthrown in 1974 in a military coup by the Derg, a Marxist-Leninist junta. The following year he was assassinated. While the state media reported at the time that he had died as a result of respiratory failure following prostate surgery, in 1994 an Ethiopian court found a number of former military officers guilty of strangling him in his bed. Selassie's removal ended one of the longest-lasting monarchies in history.

President of Bangladesh Assassinated

1975   Sheikh Mujibur Rahman, the president of Bangladesh, was killed, along with most of his family, at his home by members of the Bangladesh Army during a coup in 1975.

SS *Edmund Fitzgerald*

1975   The SS *Edmund Fitzgerald*, an American Great Lakes freighter, lost its entire crew of twenty-nine when it sank in Lake Superior during a storm in November 1975. At the time of her launch in 1958, the *Edmund Fitzgerald* was the largest ship on the Great Lakes.

President Ford Assassination Attempts

1975   President Gerald Ford survived two assassination attempts in 1975. One was by Lynette "Squeaky" Fromme, a follower of Charles Manson, who fired a Colt .45 at Ford in Sacramento, California. Fromme was convicted of attempted assassination and served thirty-four years in prison. The second attempt was in San Francisco seventeen days later. As Ford was leaving his hotel, Sara Jane Moore fired a .38-caliber revolver at the president, missing him by a few feet. She was also convicted and served thirty-two years in prison.

Tenerife Airport Disaster

1977　In March of 1977, two Boeing 747s collided on a runway at Los Rodeos Airport in Tenerife, Canary Islands. Heavy fog was the cause of the crash, which killed 583 people and is the worst aviation accident in history.

Jonestown

1978　The Reverend Jim Jones set up Jonestown, a utopian Marxist commune, in the Guyana jungle in 1977. Hundreds of devoted followers from his cult-based People's Temple in San Francisco went with him. After allegations emerged that Jones was subjecting many of his followers to sexual and physical abuse, a congressional committee and journalists arrived in Guyana in 1978 to investigate. But when they, and some of Jones's followers, tried to leave, they were shot at by Jones's guards. Jones then ordered everyone at the commune to commit suicide, encouraging or forcing them to drink a fruit punch laced with cyanide. Over nine hundred people died, including Jones, who shot himself.

American Airlines Flight 191

1979　American Airlines Flight 191 lost one of its engines during takeoff from Chicago's O'Hare International Airport in 1979. It crashed, killing all 271 people on board, as well two others on the ground. It is the deadliest single plane crash on American soil in history.

Three Mile Island

1979　In March 1979, the Three Mile Island Unit 2 reactor in Pennsylvania partially melted, releasing radioactive gases and iodine into the air. With a cleanup cost of around $1 billion, it remains the most significant nuclear power plant accident in American history.

The Disco Ball

1970   With disco music taking off in the 1970s, the mainstay of dance floors was the disco ball, a spherical ball that hung from the ceiling and reflected light in many directions. The Kentucky company Omega National Products is said to have produced most of these mirrored balls.

Platform Shoes

1972   Platform shoes made a resurgence in the early 1970s, worn by the English singer David Bowie and various punk rock artists.

Pet Rocks

1975   American advertising executive Gary Dahl marketed smooth stones from Mexico as "live" pets. He had the rocks painted and fake eyes were stuck to them. The rocks were sold for four dollars each, and over one million were sold, making him a millionaire.

Mohawk Hair

1976   With the explosion of punk rock, the Mohawk hairstyle came back into fashion in the 1970s, often sported by the punk rock band members and their followers.

1. Which Asian war began in 1971?

2. What disaster struck Guatemala and Honduras in 1976?

3. What significant event happened to the governor of Alabama, George Wallace, in 1972?

4. Developed in the 1970s, what transformed the communications industry?

5. Which Jamaican singer in the 1970s was considered the pioneer of reggae music?

6. For his role in which 1975 film did Jack Nicholson win an Academy Award for Best Actor?

7. What American comedy-drama television series from the 1970s was centered around the Korean War?

8. *Asteroids*, *Pong*, and *Breakout* were popular 1970s forms of what?

9. Which American athlete won the decathlon at the 1976 Montreal Olympic Games?

10. Which golfer won eight majors during the 1970s?

1. Indo-Pakistani War **2.** earthquake **3.** Wallace was the subject of an assassination attempt **4.** fiber optics **5.** Bob Marley **6.** *One Flew Over the Cuckoo's Nest* **7.** *M*A*S*H* **8.** video games **9.** Bruce Jenner **10.** Jack Nicklaus

THE GREED DECADE

The eighties are famous for many things, not least the collapse of European communism and the end of the Cold War. Politically, the decade saw the rise of conservatism led by Ronald Reagan in the United States and Margaret Thatcher in the UK, and a trend toward laissez-faire capitalism in an era known for money and greed. Multinational corporations proliferated, but the bloodshed across the globe in terms of wars and civil unrest continued. Despite this, global population growth in the decade was enormous and reached a level not seen before or since. And while big hair and extreme fashions permeated American life, advancements in mainstream computer technology, a swathe of blockbuster films, as well as the birth of MTV and a new generation of music reshaped the face of pop culture, leaving a stamp that would last until the present day. Arguably the most famous and talked-about decade of them all, the 1980s saw the first of the Generation Ys, also known as the millennials, enter the world.

Walkmans and Boom Boxes

1980 While these two music devices were introduced in the 1970s, it was during the eighties that the Sony Walkman and boom box players achieved enormous popularity, influencing youth culture throughout the decade and seemingly featuring in every film and television commercial.

Big Hair and Acid-Washed Jeans

1980 Big hair was the order of the day during the 1980s, with hair spray, mousse, bright colors, and perms a common theme. Meanwhile, people started wearing acid-washed jeans and leg warmers, while miniskirts returned to popularity. Many women wore shoulder pads as Joan Collins had in *Dynasty*, as well as brighter, heavier makeup. Athletic headbands, like the one worn by Mark Knopfler of Dire Straits, also came into fashion.

Generation Y

1989 The 1980s experienced arguably the biggest world population growth in history. The population of the United States in 1980 was around 226 million, and by 1989 it was about 250 million.

The Law of Averages

1989 Inflation in the United States in 1980 peaked at almost 15 percent, before dropping by the middle of the decade, only to increase to almost 5 percent by the end. The minimum wage went to $3.10 an hour in 1980 and to $3.80 by the end of the decade. A McDonald's Big Mac value pack cost $2.59 in 1985. The average price of a gallon of gas was at its highest in the decade in 1981 when it peaked at $1.31.

House prices rose only 8 percent in the 1980s compared with 43 percent in the seventies. In 1980, the average price of a new home was about $47,000.

IT'S A POLITICAL THING

Reagan to Power

1980   Former Hollywood actor Ronald Reagan became the fortieth president of the United States in 1980 and served two terms. He was tough on the "war on drugs" and took a hard line against the spread of communism. In 1987, he and Soviet leader Mikhail Gorbachev signed the Intermediate-Range Nuclear Forces (INF) Treaty to reduce nuclear missiles.

Iran-Iraq War

1980   Lasting from 1980 until 1988, a war raged between Iran and Iraq. Iran was more deeply impacted—it had to call up fifteen-year-olds as soldiers. More than one million people died in the conflict.

Mugabe to Power

1980   After being ruled by the white minority since its formation, Robert Mugabe was elected the first Black president of Zimbabwe (formerly Rhodesia).

Operation Opera

1981   Also known as Operation Babylon, in June of 1981 the Israeli Air Force launched a surprise airstrike that destroyed an incomplete Iraqi nuclear reactor.

The Falklands

1982   The British ownership of the Falkland Islands in the South Pacific had been long disputed by Argentina, and in April 1982, the Argentine Army invaded the islands. Britain sent in troops to protect its interests, and after two months of fighting, the Argentineans surrendered.

Independence from Britain

1982   Canada gained sanctioned independence from the United Kingdom in 1982. The same occurred in Australia in 1986, although the queen was retained as head of state in "the Land Down Under." New Zealand gained its independence from Britain in that same year. Zimbabwe gained independence from Britain in 1980.

Lebanon Invaded

1982   Israeli troops invaded Lebanon to attack the Palestine Liberation Organization forces that were based there. After two months of fighting, a ceasefire was called and the PLO moved to Tunisia.

Grenada Invaded

1983   In October of 1983, the United States invaded the Caribbean island of Grenada to oust the Revolutionary Military Council. The invasion was successful and resulted in the appointment of an interim government before elections were held the following year.

Civil War in Sri Lanka

1983   A civil war began in Sri Lanka in 1983 that lasted twenty-six years. It was between the majority Sinhalese people and the Tamils, who wanted to establish their own state. The government eventually defeated the rebel Tamil Tigers, but not before about 700,000 people had died in the conflict.

British Miners' Strike

1984   British coal miners went on strike for more than a year in protest over low pay and the planned closure of mines. Margaret Thatcher, the British prime minister, refused to give into their demands, and the miners eventually went back to work.

Brazilian Democracy

1985   Brazil became a democracy again after twenty-one years of military dictatorship.

The Wall Falls

1989   In November of 1989, after a number of incidents that led to the fall of the government in the East, the Berlin Wall was torn down by thousands of people from both sides, marking an end to communism in Europe. The fall of the wall followed a number of countries moving away from communism after Mikhail Gorbachev, the Soviet leader, with his policies of glasnost (openness) and perestroika (restructuring), gave the countries of the Warsaw Pact the opportunity to choose their own governments. Poland and Czechoslovakia both moved away from communism, while Romania's communist regime was overturned in a violent uprising at the end of 1989.

Tiananmen Square

1989   After allowing pro-democracy protests to go ahead in Beijing, the Chinese government later sent in tanks to stop the demonstration. This led to hundreds of people being killed and gave birth to one of the most iconic images in history—a Chinese student standing in front of a tank, blocking its path and refusing to move.

A SCIENTIFIC WORLD

Voyager

1980 *Voyager* and *Voyager 2* are American interplanetary probes that began exploring the solar system during the 1980s. They flew by Saturn in 1980, Uranus in 1986, and Neptune in 1989. Both probes have left the solar system and, as late as mid-2022, continue to operate and send back signals to Earth.

Space Shuttle

1981 The space shuttle *Columbia*, the first-ever reusable spacecraft, was launched by the United States in April of 1981.

The CD

1982 The compact disc was released in October of 1982, and in that year Sony released the world's first commercial compact disc player, the CDP-101. It cost $674, and individual CDs cost fifteen dollars.

Artificial Heart

1982 The world's first artificial heart was invented by Dr. Robert Jarvik in 1982. In December of that year it was successfully implanted into Barney Clark at the University of Utah. Clark survived for 112 days with the heart.

Home Computers

1982   The 1980s saw home computers become very popular. The Commodore 64, which was released in 1982, holds the Guinness World Record for the highest-selling single computer model of all time. Its predecessor was the Commodore VIC-20.

Camcorders

1983   Sony released the first camcorder for the consumer market in 1983. It was a Betamax camera. Then in 1985, Panasonic released the first VHS camcorder, which was preferred and came to dominate the market.

Halley's Comet

1986   Halley's Comet was visible with the naked eye in 1986 for the first time in seventy-five years.

Surrogate Pregnancies

1986   The first surrogate pregnancy, in which the woman carrying the child is unrelated to it, occurred in April of 1986 in Michigan.

Prozac

1987   The antidepressant drug Prozac was introduced in 1987, and by 1989, some pharmacies were filling tens of thousands of prescriptions every month.

Designer Babies

1989   The first "designer babies" were created in 1989 by a process where a baby's genetic makeup is selected or altered. They were a pair of female twins whose gender was selected in a laboratory.

The Eighties

1980   With the increase in pop and electronic music and the use of synthesizers, no decade of music is more talked about or played to this day than that of the eighties.

Lennon Dies (As Do Others)

1980   In December of 1980, Beatle John Lennon was shot and killed outside his home in the Dakota building in New York City by Mark David Chapman. Bob Marley died from a skin melanoma in 1981. Harry Chapin died in a car crash in 1981, and Marvin Gaye was fatally shot by his father at his Los Angeles home in 1984. Karen Carpenter died of heart failure in 1983, while Andy Gibb of the Bee Gees died in 1988 from myocarditis.

MTV

1981   The American cable channel MTV was launched in 1981. Originally showcasing only music videos, the first words spoken on the channel were "Ladies and gentlemen, rock and roll." The first music video played was "Video Killed the Radio Star" by the Buggles.

Queen

1981   Formed in London in 1970, the rock band Queen, led by flamboyant singer Freddie Mercury, released their *Greatest Hits* album in 1981. It is the best-selling album in British history and is certified nine times platinum in the United States.

Thriller

1982   Michael Jackson's 1982 album *Thriller* topped the charts and became the biggest-selling album of all time, with over sixty million sales worldwide. Jackson became an icon of the decade, known for his leather jacket, white glove, and dance moves, including the moonwalk. His 1987 album *Bad* sold over forty-five million copies, and by the end of the decade, Jackson had the most number one singles and had spent the most weeks at number one. Jackson went on to sell over one billion records.

Purple Rain

1984   Prince was one of the best-selling music artists of the decade with his album *Purple Rain* selling over 25 million copies and producing two number one singles: "When Doves Cry" and " Let's Go Crazy."

Like a Virgin

1984   The American singer Madonna released her album *Like a Virgin* in 1984, propelling her to international stardom. The "Material Girl" has sold over three hundred million records, making her the best-selling female artist of all time. Along with Whitney Houston, she was the most popular female artist of the decade.

Born in the USA

1984   After achieving worldwide fame with his 1975 album *Born to Run*, it was Bruce Springsteen's *Born in the USA* album in 1984 that propelled "the Boss" into a different league. Seven of the album's singles reached the top ten, and it is one of the best-selling albums of all time. Springsteen has now sold more than 150 million records and is ranked twenty-third on *Rolling Stone*'s Greatest Artists of All Time.

Hard Rock and Heavy Metal

1985   The decade also saw hard rock and heavy metal music dominate, with bands such as Bon Jovi, Iron Maiden, Poison, Metallica, and Guns N' Roses, the latter of which was formed in 1985. Other rock bands that achieved success in the eighties were AC/DC, Talking Heads, and the Irish band U2.

Live Aid

1985   To help the starving people of Africa, who were ravaged by drought in the early 1980s, Irish pop singer Bob Geldof arranged a group of famous musicians to record the charity single "Do They Know It's Christmas?" Then, with the Live Aid concerts in 1985, he raised over £50 million.

Hip-Hop

1989   The end of the decade introduced hip-hop music, with acts such as Run-DMC, the Beastie Boys, Public Enemy, and Tone Lōc.

Best-Selling Books

1989   The best-selling books of the decade were *The Covenant* by James A. Michener, *The Bourne Identity* by Robert Ludlum, *Rage of Angels* by Sidney Sheldon, and *Firestarter* by Stephen King.

A SPORTING LIFE

Gretzky

1984   Known as "The Great One," Canadian hockey player Wayne Gretzky dominated the NHL with his team the Edmonton Oilers, winning four Stanley Cup championships in 1984, 1985, 1987, and

1988. In 1988, Gretzky was involved in the biggest trade in NHL history, known as "The Trade of the Century," when he was sent to the Los Angeles Kings.

WrestleMania

1985   The first WrestleMania was presented by WWF (the World Wrestling Federation) in 1985 at Madison Square Garden in New York City. Over 19,000 people attended. Then, in 1987, WrestleMania II had a record attendance of over 93,000.

The Bear Is Back

1986   American golfer Jack Nicklaus, nicknamed "The Golden Bear," won a record eighteen major championships. In 1986 he won the Masters, his final major win, at the age of forty-six, the oldest player to do so.

The Goal of the Century

1986   Argentina won the 1986 FIFA World Cup held in Mexico. Diego Maradona dominated the tournament, scoring what became known as the "Goal of the Century." Often cited as the greatest individual goal of all time, he scored it in the quarter-final match against England, just four minutes after his controversial "Hand of God" goal.

Magic and Bird

1987   The two highest-profile basketball players of the decade were Magic Johnson of the LA Lakers and Larry Bird of the Boston Celtics. They competed against each other in three NBA Finals: 1984, 1985, and 1987.

Olympics

1988   The 1980 Summer Olympic Games in Moscow were boycotted by the United States and sixty-four other countries in protest of the Soviet's invasion of Afghanistan. Then the 1984 Los Angeles Games were boycotted by the Soviet Union and other communist countries in retaliation. It was those games that saw Carl Lewis burst onto the athletics scene, matching Jesse Owens's feat of winning four gold medals in the 100 meters, 200 meters, 4 x 100 meters relay, and long jump. Edwin Moses also won gold in the 400 meters hurdles, eight years after winning in Montreal. Daley Thompson of Great Britain won his second consecutive gold in the decathlon. The United States topped the medal table to win the games by a huge margin over Romania.

The Jamaican national bobsled team gained wide media attention at the 1988 Winter Olympics in Calgary, Alberta, but it was the 1988 Summer Games that produced the most famous (or infamous) sporting incident of the decade. Canadian sprinter and rival of Carl Lewis, Ben Johnson, won the 100 meters in a world record of 9.79, but he was later disqualified after testing positive for steroids. Florence Griffith Joyner also set a world record of 10.62 in the 100 meters and 21.34 in the 200 meters to win both golds.

World Series Firsts

1989   Major League Baseball was hotly contested during the 1980s with no one team dominating. The Philadelphia Phillies won their first title in 1980, while the Kansas City Royals won the World Series for the first time in 1985. The Minnesota Twins won their first World Series in 1987.

The 49ers and the Redskins

1989   Two teams dominated the Super Bowl during the decade. Under the leadership of Joe Montana, the San Francisco 49ers won four Super Bowls, while the Washington Redskins, led by head coach Joe Gibbs, won two of their three Super Bowls.

Tennis

1989   The 1980s were a golden era of tennis, both in the men's and women's games. The men were dominated by rivalries between Bjorn Borg and John McEnroe—the latter was number one from 1981 to 1984. Jimmy Connors was still competing at the highest level, while Ivan Llendl was number one from 1985 to 1987 and again in 1989. Boris Becker burst onto the scene when he won Wimbledon in 1985, at age seventeen, only to follow it up the next year. In the women's game, tennis was dominated by Chris Evert, Martina Navratilova, and Steffi Graf. Navratilova was the number one ranked player from 1982 to 1986, while Graf was number one from 1987 to 1989.

THE BIG (AND SMALL) SCREEN

Magnum PI

1980   The action series starring Tom Selleck, *Magnum PI*, ran from 1980 until 1988 and paved the way for a number of other shows to follow. These included *Knight Rider*, *The A-Team*, *The Greatest American Hero*, and *MacGyver*.

Prime-Time Soaps

1981   After the success of *Dallas* in the late 1970s, a number of soap operas were given prime-time slots in the 1980s. These included *Knots Landing*, *Dynasty*, and *Falcon Crest*.

The Smurfs

1981   A number of popular animated television shows began in the decade, including *The Smurfs* (1981), which ran for eight years; *The Transformers* (1984); and *Teenage Mutant Ninja Turtles* (1987).

E.T. the Extra-Terrestrial

1982   Directed by Steven Spielberg, the 1982 science-fiction film was the highest-grossing film of the decade and surpassed *Star Wars* as the then highest-grossing film of all time.

Letterman

1982   Television talk shows increased in popularity during the 1980s, with *The Tonight Show Starring Johnny Carson* still widely watched. *The Geraldo Rivera Show* began in 1987, but it was NBC's *Late Night with David Letterman* in 1982 that propelled the genre further. That show ran for eleven years on NBC, and then Letterman moved over to CBS with *Late Show with David Letterman*, which lasted twenty-two more years.

Cable TV

1985   By the middle of the 1980s, around 70 percent of Americans had cable television, and over 80 percent of those were paying for premium cable services.

The Brat Pack

1985   The Brat Pack was a name given to a group of young actors who appeared together in teen films during the decade. The term was first coined in 1985 (a play on "the Rat Pack"), and core members of the group included Emilio Estevez, Demi Moore, Rob Lowe, and Molly Ringwald. Two 1985 films defined the group and teen genre— *The Breakfast Club* and *St. Elmo's Fire*. *Ferris Bueller's Day Off* in 1986 and *Footloose* in 1984 were two other high-profile films in the genre.

The Blockbuster

1986   Don Simpson, producer of hits such as *Top Gun* (1986), *Beverley Hills Cop* (1984), and *Flashdance* (1983), is generally credited with starting the Hollywood blockbuster, which was one of the main film genres of the 1980s.

Action Franchises

1989   The 1980s introduced the first installments of a number of action-film franchises, including *Indiana Jones*, *Lethal Weapon*, *Die Hard*, *The Terminator*, and *Rambo*. This style of film made household names of the likes of Bruce Willis, Mel Gibson, and Arnold Schwarzenegger. Other franchises that began in the eighties were *Back to the Future* (1985), *Crocodile Dundee* (1986), and *Beverly Hills Cop* (1984).

Television Sitcoms

1989   Television sitcoms exploded in popularity in the 1980s. Shows such as *Family Ties*, *Cheers*, *The Golden Girls*, and *Married...With Children* were hugely successful. But it was *Seinfeld*, the show "about nothing" that debuted in 1989, that really changed the shape of the genre.

Martial Arts Films

1989   With action stars including Chuck Norris, Steven Seagal, and Jean-Claude Van Damme, martial arts films were very popular during the 1980s. Jackie Chan and John Woo were two of the notable martial arts filmmakers.

The Oscars

1989   The films that won the Academy Award for Best Picture during the decade, in order, were: *Ordinary People*, *Chariots of Fire*, *Gandhi*, *Terms of Endearment*, *Amadeus*, *Out of Africa*, *Platoon*, *The Last Emperor*, *Rain Man*, and *Driving Miss Daisy*.

IT'S JUST BUSINESS

Rubik's Cube

1980   Perhaps the most iconic and famous single item to come out of the eighties was the Rubik's Cube. Invented by a Hungarian architect Ernõ Rubik, it was sold by the Ideal Toy Company. Originally retailing for $1.99, it went on to become the best-selling toy in history, with over 350 million sold.

Pac-Man

1980   Video games gained in popularity in the 1980s, with *Pac-Man*, released in 1980, the highest-grossing arcade game of the decade. *Donkey Kong* and *Frogger*, both released in 1981, were two of the biggest games of the 1980s, as was *Super Mario Bros.* for Nintendo. Handheld electronic games boomed as well, with *Game & Watch* hugely popular.

Wayfarers and Aviators

1980   Propelled by films such as *Risky Business*, *The Blues Brothers*, and *Top Gun*, these two classic Ray-Ban sunglasses made a massive comeback in the 1980s.

Swatches

1983   While initially not selling well, Swatch watch sales skyrocketed in 1983, and by 1987, more than ten million had sold. The original cost was thirty-five dollars.

Black Monday

1987   In 1985, the Dow Jones rose nearly 28 percent in one year. Then on Monday, October 19, 1987, world stock markets suffered the biggest crash since 1929. The crash started in Hong Kong but spread worldwide, wiping 22 percent off the value of the Dow Jones. With prominent businessmen such as Donald Trump, and films like the 1987 classic *Wall Street*, the stock market was in the public eye during the 1980s like never before.

Apple Mac

1984   Apple released its first Macintosh computer in 1984. It was the first personal computer to utilize a mouse, and it cost $2,500.

Microsoft Windows

1985   Spearheaded by Bill Gates, Microsoft released its first Windows operating system in 1985: Windows 1.

Hyundai

1986   The Korean car manufacturer Hyundai arrived in the United States in 1986. Coupled with the Japanese cars in the market, the American companies of Chrysler, Ford, and American Motors struggled. Cars throughout the decade became more compact and efficient.

Disposable Camera

1986   Fuji released the first disposable camera in 1986. Kodak released its first disposable camera in 1987. Called "the Fling," it sold for $6.95 and could take twenty-four photos.

The Richest

1987   The richest man in the world during the 1980s was the Japanese property magnate Yoshiaki Tsutsumi. He topped the *Forbes* global wealth list three years running during the decade. At the height of his wealth in 1987, he had accumulated a $20 billion fortune.

Gameboy

1989   Nintendo released its personal gaming device Gameboy in 1989. Originally released in only Japan, it was soon available in the United States and featured *Tetris* and *Super Mario* as two of its games.

IN INFAMY

Mount St. Helens Erupts

1980   The Mount St. Helens volcano in Skamania County, Washington, erupted in May 1980, killing fifty-seven people.

President Reagan Attacked

1981   An assassination attempt was made on President Reagan when he was shot in Washington, DC, in March of 1981. The gunman was the mentally disturbed John Hinckley. Reagan's press secretary, James Brady, was also shot, resulting in severe injury, which confined him to a wheelchair from the brain damage he suffered.

Attempt on the Pope

1981   A gunman named Mehmet Ali Ağca tried to kill Pope John Paul II in Saint Peter's Square in Vatican City. The would-be assassin was sentenced to life in prison and, following the attack, the pope began traveling in a bulletproof "pope mobile."

Egyptian President Killed

1981   President Anwar Sadat, the leader of Egypt, was killed by a soldier who resented the peace deal made between Egypt and Israel.

AIDS

1983   A mystery disease that was killing people in the early 1980s was identified as Acquired Immune Deficiency Syndrome, or AIDS. Caused by the HIV virus, which attacks the person's immune system, it was responsible for the deaths of more than twenty million people.

Korean Air Lines Flight 007

1983   In September of 1983, Soviet fighter jets shot down a Korean Air Lines plane, killing all 269 people on board. Due to a navigational mistake, the aircraft flew through Soviet prohibited airspace. Thinking it was a United States spy plane, the Soviets destroyed it with air-to-air missiles. The incident created increased Cold War tensions and anti-Soviet sentiment.

Famine in Ethiopia

1983   With the lowest rainfall on record during the early 1980s, Ethiopia fell into severe famine, resulting in more than 400,000 deaths. Television images of starving children shocked the world.

Indira Gandhi Assassination

1984   Prime Minister Indira Gandhi of India ordered her troops to attack Sikh rebels in Amritsar's Golden Temple. Two hundred people died, and in an act of revenge, two of her Sikh bodyguards killed her four months later.

Japan Airlines Flight Crash

1985   In August 1985, Japan Airlines Flight 123 crashed, killing 520 people. It remains the worst single-plane crash in history. There were four survivors.

Air India Flight 182

1985   In June of 1985, Air India Flight 182 from Montreal, Canada, disintegrated in midair after a bomb planted by militant Canadian-Sikh separatists exploded. All 329 people on board, including 268 Canadian citizens, were killed. The bombing is the largest mass killing in Canadian history, and until the September 11 attacks in 2001, it was the deadliest act of airline terrorism in history.

Challenger Explodes

1986   After twenty-four successful missions, the American space program suffered a major disaster when a faulty seal caused the *Challenger* shuttle to explode just seventy-three seconds after takeoff. All seven crew members were killed.

Chernobyl

1986   Thousands were forced to evacuate the area when the Chernobyl power plant in Soviet-controlled Ukraine exploded. It was the worst nuclear disaster in history, spreading radioactive material across Europe. Forty-seven people were killed and 300,000 were displaced.

Lockerbie Bombing

1988   After Libyan terrorists planted a bomb on a plane scheduled to travel from London to New York, the bomb exploded and the wreckage crashed onto the Scottish town of Lockerbie. All 259 people on board were killed, as well as another eleven on the ground. It remains the worst terrorist attack in British history.

Drought

1988   The North American drought of 1988 and 1989 caused $60 billion in damage and the heat waves at the time killed up to 17,000 people.

Iran Air Flight 655

1988   In July of 1988, an Iran Air Flight plane was shot down by the United States' missile cruiser *USS Vincennes* over the Strait of Hormuz in the Persian Gulf. All 290 people on board were killed. The incident caused much controversy, with the crew of the *Vincennes* claiming they believed the plane was an attacking Iranian jet fighter.

Oil Spill

1989   While en route to California, the *Exxon Valdez* oil tanker ran aground off Alaska, rupturing its hull and spilling over three-quarters of a million barrels of oil. This caused great damage to the environment and killed much wildlife. The Exxon shipping company was ordered to pay nearly $1 billion in compensation.

Loma Prieta Earthquake

1989   The San Francisco Bay Area was struck by the Loma Prieta earthquake in October 1989 during Game 3 of the World Series. Sixty-five people were killed, and $13 billion in damage was caused, including the collapse of a portion of the Bay Bridge between San Francisco and Oakland.

THE WEIRD AND THE WONDERFUL

Yo-Yos Are Back

1980   Having been around commercially for decades, yo-yos made a huge comeback as a fad in the 1980s, with Coca-Cola advertising on them.

The Mullet

1980   An instantly recognizable hairstyle of the eighties, the mullet involved cutting the hair short at the front and sides but leaving it longer at the back. Famously sported by Mel Gibson in *Lethal Weapon*, it was everywhere during the decade.

Valspeak

1982   Originating in California's San Fernando Valley, the way of talking that repetitively uses words such as "like" and "totally" was brought to the mainstream in 1982 with the song "Valley Girl," which lampooned the fad.

Cabbage Patch Kids

1983   Sold for between twenty and forty dollars, the demand for Cabbage Patch Kids was so high in the Christmas of 1983 that stores across America ran out of stock.

Car Surfing

1985   Propelled by the film *Teen Wolf*, where Michael J. Fox's character stands on the roof of his friend's moving van, the fad of "surfing" on the roof of a moving vehicle took off in 1985.

Hacky Sacks

1989   The small round bags filled with pellets or sand were hugely popular in the 1980s. The idea was for players to stand in a circle, kicking the sack, with the goal of keeping it off the ground for as long as possible.

1. Which Central American country had a civil war that began in 1980?

2. Which African country was subjected to a number of military coups during the decade?

3. Name one Caribbean country that gained independence in the 1980s.

4. What was the name of the 1984 supergroup formed to raise money for Ethiopia?

5. Which actor starred in three *James Bond* films during the eighties?

6. Beginning in 1985 and starring Kirk Cameron, which American sitcom ran for seven seasons?

7. Which American diver won back-to-back gold medals in two events in the 1988 Olympics despite suffering a concussion after striking his head on the springboard?

8. Famous as a professional wrestler and American actor and starring in one of the *Rocky* films, by what name is Laurence Tureaud better known?

9. Whose 1983 album, *She's So Unusual*, was the first debut album by a female artist to have four top-five hits?

10. Which famous American actor's first role was a part in the 1981 film *Endless Love*?

9. Cyndi Lauper 10. Tom Cruise
4. Band Aid 5. Roger Moore 6. *Growing Pains* 7. Greg Louganis 8. Mr. T
1. El Salvador 2. Nigeria 3. Antigua and Barbuda, Belize, Saint Kitts and Nevis

1990s

THE GOOD DECADE

Sometimes referred to as the "Good Decade," the 1990s saw vast advancements in computer technology. With the development of the World Wide Web and the frenzy of the dot-com bubble, the world would never be the same again. Other technologies pushed forward as well, such as genetics, with cloning and designer babies. The decade also witnessed the end of the Soviet Union and the Cold War, although the news was dominated by a number of bloody conflicts in Europe, as well as domestic troubles in the US with headline events such as the LA riots, the Oklahoma bombing, and the Unabomber. Music changed from the upbeat sounds of the eighties to genres such as grunge and hip-hop, while American television was dominated by sitcoms like *Friends* and *Seinfeld*. And as the babies of the decade changed from Generation Y to Gen Z, known as "zoomers," the final decade of the twentieth century had arrived, with new-millennium fever soon to erupt.

Year of the Woman

1992   This was popularly referred to as the "Year of the Woman" after a number of female senators were elected in the United States. The decade saw the furtherance of women's rights generally, and in 1994 the Violence Against Women Act was passed.

Global Warming

1992   Global warming became an increasing concern for many people during the decade, and from 1992, the United Nations Framework Convention on Climate Change (UNFCCC) held annual summits.

Flannels and Curtained Hair

1995   The grunge music movement greatly influenced fashion during the 1990s, with Dr. Martens boots, flannel shirts, and curtained hairstyles popular among young men. Baggy jeans and baseball caps were also popular, as were tattoos and piercings for both sexes. Millions of women got "the Rachel," a hairstyle worn by Jennifer Aniston on the television show *Friends*, while bleached-blonde hair was also commonplace.

Growth

1995   The 1990s ushered in steady economic growth for much of the world, except for the former members of the Soviet Union, whose economies contracted. Inflation in the United States was over 5 percent at the start of the decade, falling to just over 2 percent in 1999. The nineties brought prosperity to the US, mainly owing to the internet and technological boom, and the Dow Jones increased markedly during the decade in what economist Alan Greenspan termed "irrational exuberance."

Generation Z

1999   In the 1990s, the world's population increased from 5.3 billion at the start of the decade to over six billion by the end. In the United States, there were almost 249 million Americans in 1990, reaching 279 million by the end of the decade.

The Law of Averages

1999   The average family income rose from $50,200 in 1990 to $54,000 by 1999, while the average price of a gallon of gas only rose from $1.15 in 1990 to $1.17 in 1999. The minimum wage was $3.80 an hour in 1990, and by 1997 it was at $5.15 an hour.

IT'S A POLITICAL THING

Gulf War

1990   In retaliation to Iraqi leader Saddam Hussein ordering his troops to invade Kuwait and seize its oil reserves, the United States intervened, beginning with the deployment of naval vessels and then escalating. The Iraqi troops were forced out.

Nelson Mandela

1990   After twenty-six years in jail in South Africa, Nelson Mandela, the anti-apartheid leader, was finally released. He returned to politics and became the head of the African National Congress. He was awarded the Nobel Peace Prize in 1993, and in 1994 he became president of South Africa, uniting the country. In that same year,

South Africa adopted a new multicolored flag, with colors representing the African National Congress, as well as the Netherlands and Britain, South Africa's colonial rulers.

Soviet Union Ends

1991   After the fall of the Berlin Wall in 1989, 1990 brought about a further decline of communism. In March of that year, free elections were held in East Germany with the voters rejecting communism. Then in October, East and West Germany were reunified. Communism was also rejected in Yugoslavia; then in December of 1991, Mikhail Gorbachev resigned; and after forty years as one of the world's two superpowers, the Soviet Union officially ceased to exist. It split into fifteen separate countries, with the Russian Federation the largest and most powerful country to emerge. Boris Yeltsin became its first president.

War in Yugoslavia

1991   After communism was rejected in the six republics making up Yugoslavia, a bloody war ensued. Four of the states, Macedonia, Croatia, Slovenia, and Bosnia and Herzegovina, tried to become independent countries, but Serbia, bent on creating a "Greater Serbia," waged war. In 1992, Bosnia and Herzegovina declared itself independent, a move that was rejected by the Bosnian Serbs. The president of Serbia, Slobodan Milošević, supported the Bosnian Serbs and, in a policy of ethnic cleansing, violently removed non-Serbs. There was a siege of the Bosnian city of Sarajevo, which was ended in 1995 after NATO air strikes. A peace deal was signed, but over 11,000 civilians had died.

European Union

1992   The Maastricht Treaty was signed in 1992, formalizing the coming together of Western European countries. This created the European Union.

Oslo Accords

1993   After secret talks in Oslo, Norway, in which the Palestine Liberation Organization agreed to end violence and recognize Israel's right to exist, and Israel agreed to withdraw from some of Palestine's territory, a peace deal was reached. The leader of the PLO, Yasser Arafat, and Israel's leader, Yitzhak Rabin, shook hands on the deal while President Bill Clinton looked on.

Massacre in Rwanda

1994   In 1994, the Hutu ethnic group attacked their rivals, the Tutsis in Rwanda. The attack was prompted by the assassination of the Hutu president, Juvénal Habyarimana. Enormous bloodshed resulted, with over 800,000 people, or 20 percent of the entire population, killed.

Haiti Invasion

1994   After being overthrown in a military coup in 1991, Haiti's first elected president, Jean-Bertrand Aristide, was returned to power with the help of United States troops in 1994.

Chechen War

1994   When the Chechnyan region attempted to break away from Russia, it was met with strong resistance. But a ceasefire in 1996 resulted in independence for Chechnya.

Cannabis Legalized

1996   Proposition 215 was passed in California in 1996, which legalized cannabis for medicinal purposes.

Congo Wars

1996   The first Congo war began in 1996 and ended thirty-two years of dictatorship in Zaire, which was renamed the Democratic Republic of the Congo. The second Congo war, which was far more devastating than the first, began in 1998 and ended in 2003.

Hong Kong Back to China

1997   In July of 1997, the United Kingdom handed sovereignty of Hong Kong to the People's Republic of China.

Clinton and Lewinsky

1998   After President Bill Clinton was caught in a scandal as a result of alleged "sexual relations" with White House intern Monica Lewinsky, he was impeached in 1998 for perjury under oath. After an investigation by federal prosecutor Kenneth Starr, the Senate acquitted Clinton and he finished his second term as president.

The Kosovo War

1998   In an attempt to prevent the Serbian region of Kosovo from becoming independent, the president of Serbia, Slobodan Milošević, sent in troops. But the Serbs were forced back by NATO air strikes, and Kosovo declared independence in 2008.

Irish Peace

1998   A treaty was signed in Ireland when the nationalist and unionist political parties agreed to serve in a power-sharing government. Known as the "Good Friday Agreement," it ended thirty years of fighting and turmoil.

Putin Leads Russia

1999   Boris Yeltsin resigned as president of Russia in 1999, making way for Vladimir Putin.

A SCIENTIFIC WORLD

World Wide Web

1990   British computer researcher Tim Berners-Lee developed a simple way of distributing computer information using hyperlinks. He called it the "World Wide Web." It was initially used by only a few people, but with the advent of internet browsers in 1993, its popularity boomed.

Hubble

1990   The American Hubble Space Telescope was sent into orbit around the Earth in 1990. The project was a success, with the telescope taking detailed images of the universe.

Mummy Found

1991   Two German tourists found a mummified Copper Age man in a glacier in the Alps. The mummified man was thought to have lived and died over 5,200 years ago and was dubbed Ötzi the Iceman.

GPS

1993   The full suite of twenty-four satellites to provide the global positioning system, or GPS, became operational in 1993. Owned by the US government and operated by the United States Air Force, the US secretary of defense opened the system to civilian use in 1993.

International Space Station

1993   Construction began on the International Space Station in 1993. Its first long-term residents arrived in November 2000.

Genetically Modified Foods

1994   Genetically modified foods went on commercial sale in 1994 and began with the delayed-ripening tomato.

DVDs

1996   DVDs—digital video discs—were released in Japan in 1996 and then in the United States in 1997. They eventually replaced prerecorded videotapes.

Hello, Dolly

1996   British scientists successfully cloned an adult mammal for the first time in 1996. The clone was an exact copy of her parent sheep and was known as "Dolly."

Pathfinder

1997   The NASA spacecraft *Pathfinder* landed on Mars, and its roving vehicle, *Sojourner*, began exploring the planet.

Instant Messenger

1997   AOL Instant Messenger was launched in 1997. It gained 53 million users in under ten years.

MP3 Players

1998   Manufactured by the South Korean company SaeHan Information Systems, MPMan was the first portable digital music player, released in 1998. MP3s are compressed computer files that store audio. Prior to this format, reproducing sound required motion, such as the spinning of a disc or a cylinder.

Camera Phones

1999   The first camera phone, called the Kyocera Visual Phone VP-210, was released in Japan in 1999.

MUSIC AND THE ARTS

Friends in Low Places

1990   Country music exploded in popularity in the 1990s, with Garth Brooks breaking all records in terms of sales and concert attendances. Many others rode the country wave during the decade, including Shania Twain, Tim McGraw, LeAnn Rimes, George Strait, and Kenny Chesney.

Grunge

1991   Beginning in Oregon and Washington State, grunge music became extremely popular in the early 1990s, with bands including Nirvana, Soundgarden, and Pearl Jam. The suicide of Kurt Cobain, the front man of Nirvana, in 1994 at the age of twenty-seven, was the start of the decline of the genre.

Alternative Rock

1991   Led by bands including the Red Hot Chili Peppers, Hootie & the Blowfish, Counting Crows, and the Smashing Pumpkins, alternative rock reached mainstream popularity early in the decade.

The Firm

1991   American writer John Grisham was the best-selling author in the United States during the decade, with his breakout novel, *The Firm*, published in 1991. With others including *The Pelican Brief*, *The Client*, *The Chamber*, *The Rainmaker*, and *The Runaway Jury*, he sold over sixty million books.

Gangsta Rap

1992   Led by Dr. Dre's 1992 album *The Chronic*, gangster rap took off early in the decade, with artists including Snoop Dogg, Ice Cube, LL Cool J, OutKast, Puff Daddy (as he was known at the time), and Eminem.

Jagged Little Pill

1995   The decade hosted a revival of female singer-songwriter artists, with success by Norah Jones, Dido, Sheryl Crow, and most notably, Alanis Morissette, with her multiplatinum 1995 album *Jagged Little Pill*.

Rap Artists Killed

1996   In September of 1996, the rap music artist Tupac Shakur was shot and killed in Las Vegas. Then, in March 1997, the Notorious B.I.G. was shot dead in Los Angeles. Neither killer was identified.

Versace Murdered

1997   Famous Italian fashion designer Giovanni Versace was shot and killed outside his Miami Beach home by Andrew Cunanan, a man on a killing spree, who also shot and killed real estate developer Lee Miglin. Cunanan killed himself eight days after he murdered Versace.

Harry Potter

1997   *Harry Potter and the Philosopher's Stone*, the first of J. K. Rowling's famous books, was published in 1997 after many rejections from publishers. The book was an instant success, and the series, comprising seven books, has sold more than five hundred million copies, making Rowling the richest woman in Britain, surpassing Queen Elizabeth II. The books have also been translated into eighty different languages.

John Denver Dies

1997   American singer-songwriter John Denver died in October of 1997 when the plane he was flying crashed into Monterey Bay near Pacific Grove, California.

Goodbye, Frank

1998   Legendary American crooner Frank Sinatra died in May of 1998, aged eighty-two. He had been plagued with illness, including pneumonia and bladder cancer and had suffered two recent heart attacks. He died at a medical center in Los Angeles, and the night after his death, the lights on the Empire State Building in New York City were turned blue, and the lights on the Las Vegas Strip were dimmed. Gregory Peck, Tony Bennett, and Frank Sinatra Jr. spoke at the funeral.

Pop Music

1999   As it had in the 1980s, pop music continued to dominate the charts during the nineties, with singers such as Celine Dion and Britney Spears. Madonna continued her chart dominance, and the Spice Girls broke into the American market and became the most successful British group in North America since the Beatles. Celine Dion's 1997 single "My Heart Will Go On" from the *Titanic* soundtrack sold an estimated eighteen million copies and became the second best-selling single by a female artist in history, only surpassed by Whitney Houston's 1992 single "I Will Always Love You," which sold twenty million copies.

Mariah

1999   Mariah Carey was named by *Billboard* magazine as the "Artist of the Decade" in the United States. With sales of over 220 million records, she is one of the best-selling music artists of all time.

A SPORTING LIFE

Atlanta Braves

1991   The 1991 World Series saw the Atlanta Braves take on the Minnesota Twins, teams that had finished last in their divisions the year before. The Twins won in the seventh game, and it has been called the greatest World Series in history. Then, in 1993, Joe Carter hit a home run for the Blue Jays as they won their second consecutive World Series.

Air Jordan

1991   In the 1990s, Michael Jordan become the most famous basketball player of all time, leading the Chicago Bulls to six NBA titles during the decade. Jordan became a major sporting icon, with high-profile marketing deals with companies such as Nike, McDonald's, and Gatorade.

Olympics

1992   The 1992 Summer Olympic Games in Barcelona, Spain, were the first that were not boycotted by any nation in twenty years. After a thirty-two-year ban, South Africa also participated in the games. The Unified Team (made up of fifteen former Soviet republics) topped the medal table, closely followed by the United States. With NBA players allowed to participate, the so-called United States "Dream Team" formed. Featuring Michael Jordan, Larry Bird, and Magic Johnson, they won gold and have been described as the greatest sports team ever assembled.

Marking one hundred years since the first modern Olympics, the 1996 games were held in Atlanta. The United States topped the medal tally, and the US women's gymnastics team, dubbed "The Magnificent Seven," won their first-ever gold medal. The Jamaican-Canadian sprinter Donovan Bailey won the men's 100 meters, in a time of 9.84. The games will also be remembered for Muhammad Ali lighting the torch. He was given a gold medal, replacing the one he had thrown into the Ohio River in 1960 after winning gold at the Rome Olympics.

In Winter Olympics controversy, figure skater Nancy Kerrigan was attacked during practice by someone hired by the former husband of Kerrigan's rival, Tonya Harding. The attack was motivated to give Harding a greater chance of winning gold at the 1994 Winter Olympics. Harding was banned for life because of her involvement in the incident.

The Cowboys and the Broncos

1992   The two most successful NFL teams of the nineties were the Dallas Cowboys and the Denver Broncos. The Cowboys won three Super Bowls in the first half of the decade, while the Broncos won their first two Super Bowls in 1997 and 1998.

Baseball Strike

1994   Major League Baseball players went on strike in August of 1994. This ended the season for the year, and the World Series was cancelled for the first time in ninety years. The strike lasted until March 1995.

Formula One

1994   Triple World Champion Ayrton Senna was killed in a crash at the San Marino Grand Prix in 1994. In that same year, Michael Schumacher began his career, winning his first two championships in 1994 and 1995.

Brazil Takes Four

1994   Brazil won the biggest event in soccer, the FIFA World Cup, in 1994, making them the first team in history to win the event four times. The final was held in California, with Brazil beating Italy on penalties.

Iron Mike Takes a Bite

1997   Considered one of the best heavyweight boxers of all time, Mike Tyson became the youngest heavyweight champion in history when he knocked out Trevor Berbick in 1986. He was also the first heavyweight boxer to simultaneously hold the WBA, WBC, and IBF titles, but his career was marked with controversy. In 1992 he was convicted of rape and sentenced to six years in prison. He was released after three years. He made a comeback and lost to Evander Holyfield in 1996. But it was their 1997 rematch that made international headlines when Tyson was disqualified for biting off a piece of Holyfield's ear.

Lance Armstrong

1999　American cyclist Lance Armstrong won the first of his seven consecutive Tour de France titles in 1999, just two years after overcoming testicular cancer. After strenuously denying doping allegations for years, in 2013 he admitted to doping and was stripped of his Tour de France titles.

Tennis

1999　Men's tennis in the nineties was dominated by Americans, most notably Jim Courier, who won four Grand Slams in the decade, and Andre Agassi, who won five. But it was Pete Sampras who led the way, winning twelve Grand Slam titles in the decade, including four US Opens and six Wimbledon titles. The women's game was led by Steffi Graf, who won thirteen Grand Slams in the nineties, as well as Monica Seles, who won nine. But it was an unsavory incident in 1993 that marred Seles's career, when she was stabbed in the back by a man while on court, forcing her out of the game for two years.

THE BIG (AND SMALL) SCREEN

The Simpsons

1990　Premiering on Fox in 1989, by the early nineties the animated sitcom *The Simpsons* had become a worldwide success. With more than seven hundred episodes and setting the trend for the genre, it has become a cult phenomenon.

Teen Soaps

1990   *Beverly Hills, 90210* ran throughout the decade and, with its spin-off, *Melrose Place*, paved the way for a raft of teenage soap series, including *Dawson's Creek* and *Party of Five*.

Legal Dramas

1990   In the 1990s, a number of legal and police dramas hit the small screen, including *Law & Order*, which ran for twenty seasons, and *NYPD Blue*, which debuted in 1993 and ran for twelve seasons.

Seinfeld

1993   While it began in 1989, it wasn't until 1993 that the sitcom *Seinfeld*, the show "about nothing," had become a major commercial success and a cultural phenomenon, making it the most popular television show of the decade.

River Phoenix Dies

1993   American actor River Phoenix died on Halloween in 1993 from a combined overdose of heroin and cocaine, known as a speedball. He died on the sidewalk in front of The Viper Room, a Hollywood nightclub part-owned by Johnny Depp. He was only twenty-three.

Cheers

1993   The series finale of the popular sitcom *Cheers* aired in 1993, and it was the most watched television episode of the decade.

Medical Dramas

1994   Launching the career of George Clooney, *ER* debuted in 1994 and ran for fifteen seasons, with 331 episodes. It paved the way for medical dramas such as *Grey's Anatomy* in the next decade.

Cult Following

1994   Four famous films hit the cinema at the same time in 1994—*Pulp Fiction, Forrest Gump, Jurassic Park*, and *The Shawshank Redemption*, all of which would end up having cult followings.

Toy Story and Animation

1995   Pixar's *Toy Story* was the first entirely computer-animated feature film, and it revolutionized the industry. Earlier in the decade, Walt Disney Feature Animation had marked success in the genre with the likes of *Beauty and the Beast, Aladdin*, and *The Lion King*.

Titanic

1997   The 1997 James Cameron film *Titanic* dominated the film industry in the 1990s, grossing $1.8 billion worldwide and making it the then highest-grossing film of all time. It won eleven Academy Awards, tying with *Ben-Hur* for the most ever won by a film.

Baywatch

1999   This American beach-based action-drama series ran throughout the nineties to become the most watched television series in the world, with an estimated weekly audience of 1.1 billion.

Academy Awards

1999   The nineties was a decade of famous films, with the following winning Best Picture in this order: *Dances with Wolves, The Silence of* *the Lambs, Unforgiven, Schindler's List, Forrest Gump, Braveheart, The English Patient, Titanic, Shakespeare in Love,* and *American Beauty.*

IT'S JUST BUSINESS

Ronald in Russia

1990   The first McDonald's restaurant opened in Moscow in 1990, with Boris Yeltsin visiting it.

The Hummer

1992   The Hummer brand of SUV cars was first released by AM General in 1992. It weighed 10,000 pounds and got less than ten miles to the gallon.

The Super Soaker

1992   The Super Soaker was the most popular and best-selling toy of 1992, selling more than two million in that year. It could shoot water up to fifty feet.

Channel Tunnel

1994   Connecting France and England, the Channel Tunnel opened in 1994 and is the world's third-longest rail tunnel and the longest undersea tunnel.

PlayStation

1994   The home video game console PlayStation was released by Sony in Japan in 1994 and then in the United States in 1995.

Barings Bank Collapses

1995   Britain's oldest merchant bank, Barings Bank, collapsed as a result of Nick Leeson, a rogue trader who gambled in unauthorized investments. His activities resulted in losses of £800 million.

E-Commerce

1995   With the advancements of computers and the internet, many e-commerce and internet companies were founded and went on to boom in the 1990s. Yahoo was founded in 1994 and Amazon and eBay began in 1995.

Hotmail

1997   With the widespread usage of email, Microsoft acquired Hotmail in 1997 for an estimated $400 million.

Netflix

1997   The American subscription streaming service Netflix was launched in 1997. It began by mailing DVDs to consumer's homes.

The Tallest

1998   The Petronas Twin Towers in Kuala Lumpur, Malaysia, were built in 1998 and were the tallest buildings in the world for six years and still remain the tallest twin towers in the world.

Google

1998   Sometimes referred to as the "most powerful company in the world," the technological giant Google was founded in 1998 in Menlo Park, California. It now employs over 140,000 people.

iMac

1998   In 1998 Apple released the iMac, the first consumer all-in-one computer.

IN INFAMY

LA Riots

1992   After being filmed violently beating a Black suspect, Rodney King, in 1991, the police officers responsible were charged with using excessive force, but were acquitted the following year at their trial. This resulted in six days of riots in which fifty-three people were killed and 5,500 properties were set on fire.

Columbus Day

1992   The celebration of the five hundredth anniversary of Christopher Columbus discovering America was met with protests against the victimization of Native Americans.

Hurricane Andrew

1992   The Category 5 Atlantic hurricane struck Florida, Louisiana, and the Bahamas in August of 1992. At the time it was the most destructive and costliest hurricane in United States history, destroying over 60,000 homes, killing sixty-five people, and causing over $27 billion in damage.

Sicilian Mafia

1992   The Italian judge Giovanni Falcone was killed by a remote car bomb in May of 1992. He was a leading figure in the fight against organized crime. Only two months later, magistrate Paolo Borsellino, a friend and colleague of Falcone's, was killed by a car bomb in Palermo, Sicily.

World Trade Center Bombing

1993   A terrorist attack was launched on the World Trade Center when a truck bomb detonated below the North Tower. Six people were killed and over one thousand injured.

Escobar Killed

1993   The infamous Colombian drug lord, Pablo Escobar, head of the Medellín Cartel and known as the "king of cocaine," was killed in his hometown by Colombian National Police. He was forty-four years old. Escobar is believed to have been the richest criminal in history, amassing a fortune of over $30 billion. It has been said that Escobar spent $2,500 every month on rubber bands just to hold his drug money together.

The Waco Siege

1993   Using tanks and tear gas, the US Bureau of Alcohol, Tobacco, and Firearms stormed the headquarters of the Christian sect Branch Davidians in 1993. During the raid, the compound caught fire. The leader of the sect, David Koresh, was killed, but so were seventy other people, including a number of children.

Rwandan Plane Shot Down

1994   In April of 1994, a plane was shot down as it prepared to land in Rwanda. It was carrying the Rwandan president Juvénal Habyarimana and the Burundian president Cyprien Ntaryamira. The persons responsible for the act were never found or identified, but the incident sparked the First Congo War.

Oklahoma Bombing

1995   As a protest over the Waco siege, ex-military man Timothy McVeigh planted a bomb next to a government building in Oklahoma City. The explosion killed 168 people. McVeigh was executed in 2001.

O. J. Simpson

1995   Described as the "trial of the century," former NFL player O. J. Simpson went on trial for the double murder of his ex-wife Nicole Brown Simpson and her friend Ronald Goldman. In October of 1995 he was found not guilty. Ninety-five million Americans watched the verdict on television.

Midwestern Heat Wave

1995   A heat wave struck the Midwest in July of 1995, with temperatures peaking at 106°F, killing over seven hundred people in Chicago.

Trans World Airlines Flight

1996   Trans World Airlines Flight 800 exploded in midair and crashed into the Atlantic Ocean near New York in July 1996—230 people were killed in the disaster.

Unabomber Arrested

1996   Ted Kaczynski, known as the Unabomber, was arrested in 1996 and sentenced to eight consecutive life sentences with no possibility of parole. The reclusive former mathematics professor killed three people and injured twenty-three others in a nationwide bombing campaign, targeting institutions he believed were advancing technology and harming the environment. In 1995 he had sent a letter to the *New York Times* with his essay "Industrial Society and Its Future." At the point of his capture, Kaczynski had been the subject of the longest and most expensive manhunt in the history of the FBI.

The Taliban

1996   In 1996, the Taliban overthrew the Afghan government, which had been in power since 1992. The Taliban established the extremist Muslim state: the Islamic Emirate of Afghanistan. In 1999, Ahmed Ressam, an Al-Qaeda militant, was arrested for intending to bomb the Los Angeles International Airport.

Princess Diana Dies

1997   Princess Diana, the former wife of Prince Charles and mother of Princes William and Harry, died in a car crash in Paris in 1997 along with Dodi Al Fayed. Millions across the world watched her televised funeral service at Westminster Abbey.

Mother Teresa Dies

1997   The Roman Catholic nun Mother Teresa, who won the Nobel Peace Prize in 1979, died at the age of eighty-seven.

Earthquakes in Turkey

1999   With a magnitude of 7.6, the İzmit earthquake hit Turkey in a series of quakes during the summer of 1999. An estimated 17,000 people were killed and an additional 50,000 were injured.

JFK Jr. Killed

1999   John F. Kennedy Jr. and his wife Carolyn Bessette and sister-in-law Lauren Bessette were killed in July 1999 when Kennedy's private plane crashed off the coast of Martha's Vineyard.

Slap Bracelets

1990 Invented in 1983, slap bracelets became very popular with children and teenagers in the early 1990s. They were invented by Stuart Anders, who made millions from the product.

Lorena Bobbitt

1993 Lorena Bobbitt rose to fame in 1993 when she cut off her husband's penis with a knife while he was asleep in bed. In 1994 Lorena was acquitted of assault by reason of insanity.

Wonderbra

1994 First trademarked in the United States in 1955, the push-up Wonderbra was introduced to the American market in 1994.

Y2K Fears

1999 The impending new millennium spread fear throughout the world because of the idea that the change in date from 1999 to 2000 was likely to cause computers to malfunction on January first, plunging society into pandemonium. Many people stocked up on canned food and supplies, and millions of dollars were spent in upgrading computer systems. But the fears were unfounded and life went on as normal.

POP QUIZ HOT SHOT
(HINT: YOU WON'T FIND THE ANSWERS ABOVE)

1. In which 1994 action film was the phrase "Pop quiz, hot shot" said?

2. Samuel Doe, the president of which African country, was murdered by rebels in 1990?

3. Name two Major League Baseball teams that were added during the 1990s.

4. Which African nation's civil war ended in 1991 after twenty years?

5. What 1990 film starring Patrick Swayze was the highest-grossing film of that year?

6. Chuck Norris starred in what popular Western television series during the 1990s?

7. What 1998 Dixie Chicks album was certified twelve-times platinum?

8. What comet went past the sun for the first time in 4,300 years in 1997?

9. What conflict popularized the twenty-four-hour news cycle?

10. What British band featuring Chris Martin formed in 1996?

1. Speed 2. Liberia 3. Miami Marlins, Colorado Rockies, Tampa Bay Rays, Arizona Diamondbacks 4. Ethiopia 5. Ghost 6. Walker, Texas Ranger 7. Wide Open Spaces 8. Hale-Bopp 9. the Gulf War 10. Coldplay

THE NOUGHTIES

After life went on following the Y2K hysteria, the first decade of the new millennium saw a marked increase in globalization, brought about by the internet and social media, which allowed for faster and easier communication between people around the world. On a social front, the advancing technology caused people to turn toward electronic devices and away from books, while computer-generated imagery became widespread in the film industry. Musical trends changed as well, with *Billboard* magazine naming the white rapper, Eminem, the artist of the decade. And so did television styles, with reality shows becoming commonplace. But in addition to these changes and the technological advancements making the world a smaller place, the decade was primarily known for two things—the "war on terror" and the global economic crisis. The vast impact of these two very negative events justified the colloquial name of the decade, which was originally dubbed in jest—the Noughties.

Millennium Madness

2000   Millions of people around the world celebrated the new millennium with gusto. And with the turn of the century came new fashion trends as well. Large hoop earrings and bandanas became popular early in the decade, as did baseball caps, polo shirts, low-rise jeans, and crop tops. At the same time, in the wake of the 9/11 attacks, Islamophobia became more commonplace in Western society. Obesity had also become a greater concern and, at the other end of the spectrum, an obsession with looks and body shape became increasingly common, with over ten million plastic surgeries being performed each year in the United States. Botox also became popular during the decade.

Growth

2009   The world economy almost doubled in size during the 2000s. While the United States still possessed the world's largest economy, the size of its contribution dropped. The decade also saw China become an economic giant (going from the sixth largest economy to the third), and to a lesser extent, India.

Generation Z Continues

2009   The first decade of the new millennium saw the world's population increase significantly, by around 700 million people, bringing the number of people to 6.8 billion. At the beginning of the decade there were around 281 million Americans, and by the end, there were around 306 million.

A Technological World

2009   The 2000s brought vast technological advancements with many people owning smartphones and portable laptops. Email became the major form of communication, while wireless internet became widespread. The USB flash drive replaced the floppy disk, and internet commerce became commonplace.

The Law of Averages

2009   The average salary in the United States in 2000 was almost $31,000. By the end of the decade it was just under $40,000. By mid-2009 the minimum wage was $7.25 an hour.

IT'S A POLITICAL THING

George W. Bush Elected

2000   The governor of Texas and Republican candidate George W. Bush was elected for the first of his two terms as United States president in 2000, defeating Vice President Al Gore. It was the first election since 1888 in which the winning candidate lost the popular vote, and it's one of the closest elections in American history.

Netherlands Same-Sex Marriage

2001   In April of 2001, the Netherlands became the first country to legalize same-sex marriage.

Twin Towers Fall

2001   In the worst terrorist attack in American history, members of Al-Qaeda flew two domestic aircraft into New York's World Trade Center on September 11, 2001, collapsing the two iconic towers. Two other planes were hijacked, one crashing into the Pentagon and the other into a field in Pennsylvania. Nineteen members of Al-Qaeda were involved—all died. Almost three thousand innocent people were also killed. In response, the United States attacked Afghanistan, the hiding place of Al-Qaeda's leader, Osama bin Laden.

War in Iraq

2003   As part of America's "war on terror," the United States invaded Iraq in an attempt to overthrow its dictator, Saddam Hussein, whom they believed was hiding weapons of mass destruction that could be used against the West. The attack was met with much international opposition and on February 15, 2003, sparked the largest-ever worldwide anti-war protest. Hussein was captured in 2003 and put on trial for crimes against humanity. He was found guilty and executed by hanging, the footage of which was available for some time on the internet.

The Sudan

2003   Claiming they were being oppressed by the government, the Darfur region of Sudan rebelled, resulting in the death of over 300,000 people.

Reagan Dies

2004   Ronald Reagan, the fortieth president of the United States, died in June 2004 after suffering a ten-year battle with Alzheimer's disease. He received a seven-day state funeral in which over 100,000 people lined up to view the casket.

Mexican Drug War

2006   The year 2006 saw the beginning of an armed conflict between the Mexican government and the major drug cartels, resulting in the arrest of some key figures in the Gulf and Tijuana cartels. This led to more violence as cartels fought for control, and resulted in around 17,000 people being killed.

North Korea Goes Nuclear

2006   In 2006 and 2009, North Korea carried out their first two nuclear tests.

Kosovo Independent

2008   Kosovo declared its independence from Serbia in 2008, despite a number of countries refusing to recognize it. This was two years after Montenegro became independent from Serbia, ending Yugoslavia.

Obama Becomes President

2008   Democratic candidate Barack Obama was elected president of the United States in 2008 and became the first African American president in history.

South Ossetia War

2008   In response to Georgia's attack on South Ossetia, Russia invaded the nation of Georgia in August of 2008, marking the first European war of the twenty-first century. The war lasted just twelve days before a cease-fire agreement was reached.

Global Warming

2009   The World Meteorological Organization announced in 2009 that the decade was the hottest since records began in 1850 and included four of the five hottest years on record. Climate change and global warming became increasing worldwide concerns.

A SCIENTIFIC WORLD

International Space Station

2000   November 2, 2000, was the last time all living humans were on Earth at the same time. Since that date, the International Space Station has always had someone aboard.

Artificial Heart

2001   The world's first artificial heart, known as AbioCor, was implanted in 2001 into the American Robert Tools. He survived for 151 days.

Space Tourism

2001   American engineer/entrepreneur Dennis Tito became the first space tourist when he spent almost eight days in orbit on a Russian spacecraft visiting the International Space Station. The trip cost Tito $20 million.

Mars Exploration Rover

2004   The Mars Exploration Rover reached the planet in 2004 and sent data and images back to Earth.

Pluto Demoted

2006   In 2006 Pluto was demoted to a dwarf planet after seventy-six years on our solar system's planet list. This was because of the discovery of Eris, an object of similar size to Pluto.

Large Hadron Collider

2008   Built to re-create the conditions just after the big bang, this machine began operating beneath the French-Swiss border in 2008.

MUSIC AND THE ARTS

The Da Vinci Code

2003   While J. K. Rowling was the best-selling writer of the decade, it was *The Da Vinci Code*, by American author Dan Brown, that was the single best-selling book. By the end of the decade it had sold over eighty million copies.

Simon and Garfunkel Return

2003   In February 2003 Paul Simon and Art Garfunkel reunited for the first time in ten years to perform "The Sound of Silence" at the Grammy Awards.

The Man in Black Departs

2003   Johnny Cash died in Nashville in September of 2003, aged seventy-one, from complications from diabetes. His death was only four months after that of his wife June Carter-Cash. In the very last years of his life, Cash's career had experienced a resurgence, largely as a result of the Rick Rubin–produced *American Recording* albums, of which there were six. The video for his 2002 cover of the Nine Inch Nails song "Hurt" received a Grammy Award.

Hunter S. Thompson

2005   American writer and founder of gonzo journalism Hunter S. Thompson died from a self-inflicted gunshot wound to the head in Woody Creek, Colorado, in 2005. In August of that year, his ashes were fired from a cannon to the sounds of Bob Dylan's "Mr. Tambourine Man" in a prearranged private funeral. Thompson was famous for his controversial political commentaries, as well as his 1971 novel *Fear and Loathing in Las Vegas*.

Rolling Stones Go Big

2006   The 2006 Rolling Stones "A Bigger Bang" tour became the highest-grossing tour of all time, bringing in an estimated $437 million.

Hip-Hop

2009   Music of the decade was dominated by hip-hop, with artists including Eminem, Jay-Z, Kanye West, Ludacris, Gorillaz, Snoop Dogg, and 50 Cent.

R&B

2009   Alongside hip-hop, R&B music also increased in popularity with Black Eyed Peas, Alicia Keys, R. Kelly, Amy Winehouse, Jamie Foxx, and John Legend.

Music Artist of the Decade

2009   *Billboard* magazine named American rap artist Eminem (born Marshall Bruce Mathers III) as the artist of the decade. One of the best-selling artists of all time, Eminem has sold more than 220 million records. The female artist of the decade was Beyoncé.

Drawing by Raphael

2009   *Head of a Muse*, a drawing by Raphael, the Italian painter and architect during the High Renaissance, sold in an auction at Christie's, London, for just under $48 million. It was the most expensive drawing by an old master ever sold.

Goodbye, Michael Jackson (and Others)

2009   One of the most publicized trials of all time, the People v. Jackson began in 2005. Jackson was acquitted of all counts of child molestation. The entertainer died of cardiac arrest from an overdose of prescribed drugs in June 2009. Internet websites slowed down and crashed after millions of people went online to read about the news. Jackson's memorial service was streamed by over 31 million Americans, with an estimated worldwide audience of up to three billion. Other major artists to die during the decade were the "Godfather of Soul," James Brown in 2006, aged seventy-three; Ray Charles in 2004, also seventy-three; and former Beatle George Harrison in 2001. The latter died of lung cancer at the age of fifty-eight.

A SPORTING LIFE

Olympics

2000   The decade began with the Summer Olympic Games held in Sydney, Australia. The United States won the games, followed by Russia. The star of the Olympics was American sprinter Marion Jones, who won three gold and two bronze medals. But she was stripped of her medals in 2007 after admitting to steroid use. She was also sentenced to six months in prison after lying to a grand jury investigating the case. Meanwhile, Michael Johnson successfully defended his 400 meters sprint title, the only man ever to do so.

The United States also won the 2004 Olympics in Athens, followed by China. Michael Phelps hit headlines when he became the first athlete to win eight medals in these non-boycotted games. He won six gold and two bronze.

The 2008 Summer Olympics were held in Beijing, with the hosts topping the medal tally, followed by the United States. The highlight of the games was the Jamaican sprinter Usain Bolt. He became the fastest man in history, setting a new world record of 9.69 seconds for the 100 meters, and the only man in history to break three sprinting records at one Olympics—the 100 meters, 200 meters, and the 4 x 100 meters relay. In the pool, Michael Phelps dominated and won eight gold medals, more than any other athlete in a single Olympics, surpassing Mark Spitz.

Tiger Wins Three

2000   Golf during the 2000s was dominated by Tiger Woods, who won a total of twelve majors in the decade, including three of the possible four in the year 2000. In 2009 he was embroiled in scandal when it emerged that he had been involved in a number of infidelities. In November 2009, the *National Enquirer* published a story that Woods had an affair with New York City nightclub manager Rachel Uchitel. Two days later, Woods crashed his car near his home, suffering minor injuries.

Lakers Three-Peat

2002   Led by Kobe Bryant and Shaquille O'Neal, the Los Angeles Lakers won three NBA championships in a row from 2000 to 2002.

And after two seasons with the Washington Wizards, Michael Jordan retired from the NBA in 2003.

Beckham Comes to America

2007   English soccer player David Beckham joined the Los Angeles Galaxy team in 2007 as the highest-paid player in the league's history. His three-year contract was worth $6.5 million per year.

The Yankees Start and Finish

2009   The Yankees won the first and last World Series of the decade, while the Boston Red Sox won in 2004, their first World Series since 1918, and again in 2007.

Steelers Record

2009   While the New England Patriots won three Super Bowls during the decade, the Pittsburgh Steelers won two, with their 2009 victory making them the first team in history to win six titles.

Ronaldo Record

2009   Cristiano Ronaldo set the world soccer transfer record in 2009 when the Spanish club Real Madrid purchased him from Manchester United for €93 million.

Federer

2009   Roger Federer was the dominant force in men's tennis during the 2000s. He won Wimbledon in 2003 for his first Grand Slam title, and then he became the first player to win his first seven Grand Slam finals. While Rafael Nadal beat Federer for three titles, including the 2008 Wimbledon epic, the Swiss player won a total of sixteen Grand Slam titles for the decade. The women's game was dominated by the Williams sisters, with Serena winning ten Grand Slams during the decade and Venus seven, the same number as Belgian player Justine Henin.

THE BIG (AND SMALL) SCREEN

Reality Television

2000   The decade saw a boom of reality television shows, most notably *Survivor* (2000), *Big Brother* (2001), *American Idol* (2002), *The Apprentice* (2004), *Dancing with the Stars* (2005), *The Hills* (2006), *The Real Housewives of Orange County* (2006), and *Keeping Up with the Kardashians* (2007).

Drama Series

2000   Drama series were very popular during the 2000s, with *The West Wing* winning the Primetime Emmy Award four times, *The Sopranos* and *Mad Men* twice each, as well as *Lost* and *24* winning once each. Other notable dramatic series were *The Wire*, which began in 2002; *Deadwood* (2004); *Friday Night Lights* (2006); and the hugely popular and critically acclaimed *Breaking Bad* in 2008.

Comedy Continues

2000   The television sitcom genre was strong during the 2000s, with *Curb Your Enthusiasm*, written and starring *Seinfeld* cocreator Larry David, beginning in 2000; *Two and a Half Men* in 2003; *Entourage* in 2004; *How I Met Your Mother* in 2005; *30 Rock* in 2006; and *Rules of Engagement* and *The Big Bang Theory* in 2007.

Gladiator Wins

2000   The 2000 film *Gladiator* grossed over $457 million worldwide and won the Academy Award for Best Picture, as well as Best Actor for Russell Crowe. Crowe was nominated the following year for *A Beautiful Mind*, which also won Best Picture. The other films that won Best Picture during the decade were (in order): *Chicago*, *Lord of the Rings: The Return of the King*, *Million Dollar Baby*, *Crash*, *The Departed*, *No Country for Old Men*, *Slumdog Millionaire*, and *The Hurt Locker*.

Shrek and Computer Animation

2001   With the success of *Shrek* in 2001, computer-animated films gained in popularity during the 2000s, with the *Ice Age* series and *Fantastic Mr. Fox* notable works in the genre.

Prime-Time Soaps

2003   Prime-time soap operas continued to be popular during the 2000s, with *Dawson's Creek* running until 2003, *The O.C.* and *One Tree Hill* first airing in that same year, as well as *Desperate Housewives* in 2004.

Lord of the Rings

2003   The 2003 film *Lord of the Rings: The Return of the King* won eleven Academy Awards, tying *Ben-Hur* and *Titanic* for the most ever.

Fahrenheit 9/11

2004   The decade saw the rise of documentary films such as the 2004 *Super Size Me*, about eating only McDonald's food for thirty days, and the critically acclaimed *Fahrenheit 9/11* by Michael Moore. That film, which was a critical look at the presidency of George

W. Bush and the Iraq War, became the highest-grossing documentary of all time.

Avatar

2009   The 2009 science-fiction film written and directed by James Cameron became the highest-grossing film of all time, surpassing Cameron's *Titanic*, and also the first film to gross more than $2 billion.

Superheroes Are Back

2009   Superhero films made a big comeback during the decade with the likes of *X-Men*, *Batman*, *Spider-Man*, *The Incredible Hulk*, *Iron Man*, and *Fantastic Four* all in the cinemas.

Time to Switch Off

2009   A number of long-running television series aired their final episodes during the decade. *Friends* ended in 2004, the final episode being the most watched single episode of the decade in the United States with over 52 million viewers. *Frasier* ended in 2004, *That '70s Show* in 2006, and *ER* in 2009. *X-Files* ended its initial nine-season run in 2002, though it returned for two shortened seasons in 2016 and 2018.

IT'S JUST BUSINESS

PlayStation 2

2000   Released by Sony in 2000, PlayStation 2 was the best-selling video game console of the decade. More than 150 million were sold.

Segway

2001   The first Segway, a two-wheeled personal transport, hit the market in 2001.

Xbox

2001   Microsoft's first game console was released in 2001. Xbox's launch broke sales records, but it was discontinued in 2005, only to be followed by later releases.

Websites Soar

2001   A number of now enormous websites were launched in the decade, including Wikipedia, iTunes, and Google Earth in 2001, and Google Maps in 2005.

Collapse of Enron

2001   The energy giant Enron collapsed after it was discovered that it had been falsifying its accounts in order to appear more profitable.

The Dot-Com Bubble Bursts

2001   After a period of enormous growth during the late nineties, the dot-com bubble burst early in the decade, the Nasdaq Composite stock market index dropping 78 percent from its peak.

AOL and Warner

2001   AOL and Time Warner merged in 2001. The deal was valued at $350 billion, which was the largest merger in the history of the United States.

iPod

2001   In 2001 Apple launched a new breakthrough product, the iPod, which was a small, portable music device that could store and play tens of thousands of songs.

Birth of the Euro

2002   In January of 2002, seventeen European countries adopted the euro as their new joint currency, marking the end of such famous currencies as the French franc and the German deutsche mark. The euro would become the second-largest reserve currency and the second most traded currency in the world after the United States dollar.

Concorde Grounded

2003   The supersonic passenger airliner Concorde was grounded in 2003 after a downturn in demand, largely due to the plane's only crash in 2000.

Nokia's Rise and Fall

2003   The Nokia 1100 was the best-selling phone handset of the decade, with more than 250 million sold between 2003 and 2009. By the end of the decade, its sales were beginning to decline.

Google Floats

2004   In 2004 Google shares were floated on the stock market at $85 each.

Facebook

2004   Facebook, the social networking site, was launched in 2004 and by the end of the decade had over 350 million users worldwide.

Prior to its appearance, MySpace was the most popular social media site.

Nintendo DS

2004   Released in 2004, the Nintendo DS was the best-selling portable game system during the 2000s.

YouTube

2005   YouTube, the American online video-sharing platform, was launched in 2005. Now owned by Google, it is the world's second most visited website after Google itself.

Wii Sports

2006   Produced by Nintendo, Wii Sports, the sports-simulation video game, was released in the United States in November 2006.

Twitter

2006   Twitter, the social networking site, was launched by Jack Dorsey in 2006.

iPhone

2007   In 2007 Apple launched another new breakthrough product, the iPhone. Generically called a "smartphone," it had the power of early home computers. In addition to its primary use as a cell phone, it could access the internet and take photographs and videos.

MacBook Air

2008   Steve Jobs introduced the MacBook Air in 2008. It was promoted as the world's thinnest notebook.

Bernie Madoff

2008   Former chairman of the Nasdaq and owner of his own investment advisory firm, Bernie Madoff admitted to running a Ponzi scheme worth almost $65 billion. In 2009 he was sentenced to 150 years in prison, the maximum sentence permitted.

Bull Market

2007   In October of 2007, the Dow Jones closed at the record level of over 14,000, including its highest-ever intraday level of 14,198.10. This was a huge increase from the early 2006 level of 11,000.

Economic Crisis

2007   In the biggest economic crisis since the Great Depression, the world's economy collapsed in late 2007. The event was triggered by the subprime mortgage crisis, where banks had lent money for homes that many people could not afford to repay. Many banks and other financial institutions went into bankruptcy. The resultant pay cuts in Greece led to riots in the streets.

WhatsApp

2009   The instant messaging app WhatsApp was founded in 2009.

Bill Still on Top

2009   Bill Gates was the richest man in the world throughout the 2000s.

Anthrax Attacks

2001   Just one week after the September 11 terrorist attacks, letters containing anthrax spores were mailed to a number of news media offices as well as to two Democratic senators: Tom Daschle and Patrick Leahy. Five people were killed in the attacks and an additional seventeen were infected. A suspect, United States government scientist Bruce Ivins, committed suicide in 2008 before he was officially named or any guilt was proven.

American Airlines Flight 587

2001   On November 12, 2001, an American Airlines flight crashed in Queens, New York City, killing all 260 people on board and another five on the ground.

Earthquake in Gujarat

2001   An earthquake measuring 7.9 on the Richter scale hit Gujarat, a state of northwest India. More than 20,000 people were killed and 600,000 were left homeless.

Milošević on Trial

2002   The former president of Yugoslavia, Slobodan Milošević, stood trial in the International Court of Justice in the Hague, Netherlands, in 2002. He was charged with war crimes during the Bosnian War, but he died in prison before the end of the trial. In 2000 he had been overthrown after he was accused by opposition figures of rigging the election that year.

Terrorist Attacks

2002   In protest against the wars in Afghanistan and Iraq, Al-Qaeda and its related organizations launched a number of terrorist attacks against the West. In October 2002, two bombs were set off in a nightclub in Bali, Indonesia, killing over two hundred people including many Western tourists. In March 2004, bombs were set off in Madrid, Spain, killing over 190 people and injuring 1,800. In July 2005, bombs were set off on underground trains and a bus in London, killing fifty-two people and injuring over seven hundred others. In 2006, more than two hundred were killed in Mumbai, India, when bombs exploded on trains. Then, in 2008, more than 150 people were killed in Mumbai in shooting and bomb attacks. In 2007, bombs in Algiers killed over seventy people, including seventeen United Nations' staff.

Space Shuttle Columbia

2003   On February 1, 2003, the space shuttle *Columbia* disintegrated as it reentered the atmosphere, killing all seven people on board. It occurred over Texas and Louisiana and resulted in the suspension of space shuttle flights for twenty-nine months.

Tsunami

2004   On Boxing Day (December 26) in 2004, an earthquake in the Indian Ocean created an enormous tsunami more than one hundred feet in height. The wave struck fourteen countries across Asia, where it wreaked destruction and killed more than 230,000 people.

Beslan Hostage Crisis

2004   One thousand people were taken hostage by Chechen separatists who were protesting against Russian rule. The hostages were held in a school in the town of Beslan. Russian troops attempted to rescue the hostages, but it ended in disaster, with 186 children being killed.

Katrina

2005   New Orleans was devastated in 2005 when Hurricane Katrina hit. The protective levees broke under the pressure of the storm surge, flooding the city. This resulted in thousands of people becoming homeless and billions of dollars worth of damage. More than 1,800 people were killed in the disaster.

George Tiller Killed

2009   George Tiller, the American physician and late-term abortion provider, was killed by Scott Roeder, an anti-abortion extremist in 2009. Tiller was shot by Roeder while Tiller was serving as an usher at his church in Wichita. Roeder was convicted of murder and sentenced to life in prison.

Swine Flu

2009   In 2009 President Obama declared H1N1, or swine flu, a national emergency. The first two cases were discovered in the US in April of that year.

THE WEIRD AND THE WONDERFUL

Janet at the Super Bowl

2004   Sometimes referred to as "Nipplegate" but described as a "wardrobe malfunction," Janet Jackson's breast was exposed briefly by Justin Timberlake during a performance in the halftime show at the 2004 Super Bowl in Houston, Texas. The incident was viewed by around 150 million people and led to widespread debate about indecency in broadcasting.

Geek Chic

2005   By the mid-2000s a fashion trend had developed where some young people intentionally dressed like "geeks," wearing oversized, black horn-rimmed glasses and suspenders. Often the glasses had nonprescription lenses or no lenses at all. Celebrities such as Justin Timberlake and David Beckham were known to wear these sorts of spectacles.

POP QUIZ HOT SHOT
(HINT: YOU WON'T FIND THE ANSWERS ABOVE)

1. What war involving Israel began in 2006?

2. What African civil war ended in 2002 after eleven years of fighting?

3. In what South American country was the first female president elected in 2006?

4. What country experienced the deadliest bushfires in their history in 2009?

5. Who became the most decorated figure skater in American history during the 2000s?

6. Which Formula One racing driver was disqualified from the 2009 Australian Grand Prix for giving misleading evidence during a stewards' hearing?

7. What band had popular and commercial success with their 2004 album *American Idiot*?

8. Which singer had the best-selling Spanish album of the decade?

9. Who won Best Actress for her role in the 2004 film *Million Dollar Baby*?

10. With six films released during the decade, which film franchise is the third highest-grossing in history?

1. Lebanon War **2.** Sierra Leone Civil War **3.** Chile **4.** Australia **5.** Michelle Kwan **6.** Lewis Hamilton **7.** Green Day **8.** Shakira **9.** Hilary Swank **10.** Harry Potter

2000s: The Noughties　　　　　　　　**145**

2010s

THE TEN-SIONS

The twenty tens, also known as the "tens" or the "teens," began amid the global financial crisis and the continuation of the terrorist activities that had plagued the Noughties, with the rise of the Islamic State. These two factors created a great deal of unrest in many countries. While the United States remained the world's major superpower, China's world presence grew. Global warming became an even bigger issue during the course of the decade, while major natural disasters in the forms of earthquakes and tsunamis ravaged the planet. As computer technology continued to advance, smartphones became commonplace, while digital music sales topped those of CDs, and music-streaming services boomed. Online streaming services also took away market share from cable networks on the television front, while superhero films topped the box office and the best-selling book of the decade was the erotic novel *Fifty Shades of Grey*. And as Generation Alpha took their first steps, the most devastating pandemic in living memory swept the world, causing widespread death and disruption.

HIGH SOCIETY

Hipsters and Active Wear

2010 Hipster fashion saw a revival during the decade, with vintage clothing, horn-rimmed glasses, and beards quite common. Tight-fit clothing and more formal attire also became more prevalent, as did women wearing Lycra sportswear when not actually engaged in sporting activities. Normcore fashion, which involved wearing white, black, or gray clothing with no logos, also became popular, particularly among the rich, with the likes of Mark Zuckerberg and Bill Gates adopting that style.

Decline in Growth

2019 The decade began in the middle of a global financial crisis, and consumer spending remained low throughout the 2010s. Inflation in the United States also remained low for the ten-year period. By the end of the decade, China had cemented itself as a world superpower, overtaking the United States as the world's largest trading nation and moving in front of Japan to become the second-largest economy in the world. As China did, Russia, led by Vladimir Putin, also increased its military.

Generation Alpha

2019 The world's population topped seven billion in 2011 and by the end of the decade was almost 7.7 billion. With an increase in life expectancy and a fall in birth rates, a larger portion of the population of the United States was elderly.

The Law of Averages

2019   The minimum wage remained at $7.25 for the whole of the decade. The average annual wage in the United States in 2010 was almost $42,000, and in 2019 it was just over $54,000. The average price of a gallon of gas in 2010 was $2.79, and by 2019 it was down to $2.60.

IT'S A POLITICAL THING

Bin Laden Killed

2011   After ten years of searching, Osama bin Laden, leader of Al-Qaeda, was found and killed in Pakistan by an operation undertaken by United States Navy SEAL commandos.

Arab Spring

2011   Calling for greater human rights and democracy, people protested across the Arab world. The protests began in Tunisia but quickly spread to other countries, bringing war and unrest to the region.

Libya

2011   Resolution 1973 was adopted by the United Nations Security Council, which allowed for military intervention in the Libyan Civil War. A NATO-led coalition launched an air attack against Colonel Gaddafi's government. Fighting continued from March until October, when Gaddafi was captured and killed. Gaddafi's fall then led to the second Libyan civil war.

Occupy Wall Street

2011   September 2011 saw a protest movement in the United States against economic inequality and the influence of money in the political sphere. It began in Zuccotti Park in the financial district of Wall Street in New York City, where protesters set up camp. This led to the Occupy movement across the United States and the world.

Syrian War

2011   In response to protestors demanding democracy, President Assad involved the Syrian military. This quickly escalated into a civil war, with tens of thousands of deaths, resulting in a major refugee crisis.

Nelson Mandela Dies

2013   Nelson Mandela, the anti-apartheid leader and president of South Africa from 1994 to 1999, died in December 2013.

Black Lives Matter

2013   To highlight and put an end to racism and inequality for Black people, the Black Lives Matter, or BLM, movement began in 2013.

Russia in Ukraine

2014   In February of 2014, Russia took control of key places in the Ukrainian territory of Crimea and then annexed the region. This resulted in a war in the Donbas region of Ukraine.

Hong Kong Protests

2014   Known as the "Umbrella Revolution," the 2014 Hong Kong protests were a series of street demonstrations that lasted from September to December. They began after the Standing Committee of the National People's Congress made a decision about reforming the electoral system. The protests were met with police violence, including the use of tear gas.

Islamic State

2014   A new militant group emerged in Iraq in 2014 called Islamic State. Islamic State occupied the cities of Mosul in Iraq and Raqqa in Syria, but the locals fought back, supported by the United States military. By 2017, the cities had been retaken, although millions of people had been forced to flee. Islamic State also occupied Palmyra in Syria, one of the world's best-preserved archaeological sites, from 2015 to 2017. The group destroyed much of the ancient city in an effort to eradicate buildings sacred to other religions or eras.

Obergefell v. Hodges

2015   In 2015 the Supreme Court of the United States ruled that same-sex couples had a fundamental right to marry. Jim Obergefell, the American civil rights activist, was the lead plaintiff in the case. Obergefell had originally sued the state of Ohio, which had refused to legally recognize his marriage to John Arthur.

Trump Elected

2016   After Barack Obama completed his second term as president, defeating Mitt Romney in the 2012 election, Republican businessman Donald Trump defeated Hillary Clinton to become the forty-fifth president of the United States in 2016. Trump was the first United States president without any military or diplomatic experience. He implemented his "America First" policy and promised that Mexico would pay for a wall to be built on the border of the two countries.

Turkey Invades Syria

2016   In 2016, during the Syrian Civil War, Turkey invaded northern Syria to fight the Islamic State of Iraq and the Levant and the Syrian Democratic Forces.

Brexit

2016   In a referendum in 2016, the British public voted to leave the European Union after forty-three years. This became known as "Brexit," the term coined as a combination of the words "British" and "exit."

Castro Dies

2016   Former revolutionary leader of Cuba, Fidel Castro, died in 2016, aged ninety. His cause of death was not disclosed.

Philippine Drug War

2016   President Rodrigo Duterte assumed power in the Philippines in 2016 and launched a war on drugs in response to a rise in drug trafficking in the country. Over six thousand people have been killed as a result of the policy.

Nuclear Reduction

2017   In 2017, the United Nations passed a treaty prohibiting nuclear weapons, which was signed by fifty-eight countries. This followed the 2010 treaty between Russia and the United States to reduce their nuclear weapon stockpiles. Meanwhile, North Korea continued to expand its nuclear arsenal.

Mugabe Gone

2017   After leading Zimbabwe for thirty-seven years, Robert Mugabe was ousted from power by members of his party in a political coup. He was replaced with former vice president Emmerson Mnangagwa.

Women March

2017   In a demonstration for women's equality in Washington, DC, around 200,000 people marched. This march was held the day after the presidential inauguration: January 21, and many women in the crowd showed their solidarity by wearing knitted pink caps. Millions of others joined in local marches across the United States and the rest of the world.

Yellow Vests Protests

2018   The yellow vests protests were a series of mass demonstrations in France against economic injustice, with a view to increasing the minimum wage, ending austerity measures, and improving living standards. The first phase of the movement lasted over a year and involved around three million people.

Korean Leaders Meet

2018   For the first time since the end of the Korean War in 1953, the leaders of North and South Korea crossed the border, shook hands, and held peace talks.

George Bush Dies

2018   The forty-first president of the United States, George H. W. Bush, died in 2018 at the age of ninety-four. Bush died after a long battle with vascular Parkinson's disease. He served as president from 1989 to 1993 and also as vice president under Ronald Reagan from 1981 to 1989. His funeral was attended by every living former president and first lady, including the Obamas, the Clintons, the Carters, and Bush's son and daughter-in-law George W. and Laura. President Donald Trump and the first lady were also present. Countless foreign heads of state attended and paid their respects.

Chinese Leader for Life

2018 China's National People's Congress changed the constitution, allowing its leaders to stay in power indefinitely. This gave Xi Jinping the status of "leader for life."

India and Pakistan

2019 In response to a suicide car bombing that killed forty Indian security personnel, India launched airstrikes on terrorist camps in Kashmir and Pakistan.

Persian Gulf Crisis

2019 The ongoing Persian Gulf Crisis began in May 2019 when the United States increased its military presence in the region to deter an alleged planned attack against American interests in the Gulf.

Trump to North Korea

2019 President Trump met with North Korean leader Kim Jong-un at a summit at the Korean Demilitarized Zone. It was the first time a sitting United States president had set foot in North Korea since the Korean War. (Former presidents Carter and Clinton had visited North Korea after they left office.)

Trump Impeached

2019 President Trump was impeached by the House of Representatives in December of 2019 on charges of abuse of power and obstruction of Congress. He was acquitted by the Senate in February 2020.

A SCIENTIFIC WORLD

Drones

2010 Drones increased in popularity during the 2010s; they were used for aerial photography, making deliveries, and warfare.

Mobile Apps

2010 Mobile apps for smartphones were marketed commercially in 2010, primarily through app stores set up by Apple and Android.

The Shuttle Is Grounded

2011 The United States space shuttle program ended in 2011. The last flight was by space shuttle *Atlantis*.

Curiosity

2012 After an eight-month journey, the NASA research vehicle *Curiosity* landed on Mars. The rover was equipped with cameras and designed for the long-term exploration of the planet; a main goal was to determine whether Mars has ever supported life.

China Goes to the Moon

2013   China landed a spacecraft on the moon in 2013, which was the first lunar landing in thirty-seven years. Then in 2019, their *Chang'e 4* craft became the first human-built object to land on the far side of the moon.

3D Printers

2014   3D printers and scanners became commercially available by the middle of the decade. These allowed users to easily fabricate all sorts of three-dimensional objects.

Electric Cars

2015   Electric and hybrid cars became popular during the decade, and the Chevrolet Volt became the world's best-selling electric car in history, selling over 100,000 in 2015.

Event Horizon Telescope

2019   The Event Horizon Telescope, which consists of a global network of telescopes, captured the first image of a black hole, which was published in April 2019. The black hole was at the center of galaxy Messier 87.

5G

2019   Korea became the first country to use 5G broadband, but it was launched in the United States just hours later.

Country Music Resurgence

2010   With artists like Blake Shelton, Alan Jackson, Eric Church, Carrie Underwood, Jason Aldean, and Florida Georgia Line, country music gained in popularity during the 2010s.

Streaming Music

2010   Music streaming services such as Spotify and Apple Music changed the way many consumers bought and listened to music during the 2010s, with digital music sales overtaking CDs.

Pop Music

2010   Pop music surged during the decade with popular artists such as Katy Perry, Lady Gaga, Rihanna, Taylor Swift, and Justin Bieber selling over one hundred million records each.

Rock Revival

2019   After seeing somewhat of a decline during the 2000s, rock increased in popularity during the decade, moving to a softer style. A number of rock bands also made comebacks during the 2010s including Metallica, Red Hot Chili Peppers, Pearl Jam, Radiohead, and Green Day.

Artist of the Decade

2019   Canadian rapper Drake was named artist of the decade by *Billboard* magazine. Other solo acts to achieve great success were Adele, Beyoncé, Ariana Grande, Ed Sheeran, and Selena Gomez, while the groups to top the charts were One Direction, Zac Brown Band, Maroon 5, and the Lumineers.

Best-Selling Books

2019   Books remained big sellers during the decade, with the following authors topping the charts: John Grisham, Tom Clancy, James Patterson, Stephen King, and Stieg Larsson. But it was the erotic *Fifty Shades of Grey* series by E. L. James that sold the most, the three books selling a combined 34.9 million copies in the United States alone.

Whitney and Others

2019   The decade saw the death of a number of music stars, including Amy Winehouse (2011); Lou Reed (2013); Joe Cocker (2014); B.B. King and Ben E. King (2015); David Bowie, George Michael, Prince, Leonard Cohen, Merle Haggard, and Glenn Frey (all in 2016); Glen Campbell, Chuck Berry, and Tom Petty (2017); and Aretha Franklin (2018). But it was death of Whitney Houston in 2012, from an accidental drug-induced drowning in a bathtub in the Beverly Hilton hotel, that really hit the headlines.

A SPORTING LIFE

Kelly Slater Keeps on Winning

2011   In 2011 Kelly Slater won his eleventh world surfing title, making him by far the most successful surfer in the history of the sport.

Olympics

2012   The first Summer Olympic Games of the decade were held in 2012 in London, England. The United States topped the medal tally, followed by China and then the host nation. American swimmer Michael Phelps once again dominated in the pool, winning six medals, including four gold, while Usain Bolt was the star of the track once again, winning gold in the 100 meters, 200 meters, and 4 x 100 meter relay.

The 2016 Olympics in Rio de Janeiro were also won by the United States, with Great Britain second and China third. Phelps won another six medals, with five golds, making him the most successful Olympian in history. And Usain Bolt once again starred on the track, winning gold in the 100 meters, 200 meters, and 4 x 100 meter relay. With those wins, Bolt became the first athlete to win the "triple-triple"—three sprinting gold medals in three consecutive Olympics. However, in 2017 Bolt was stripped of the 4 x 100 meters gold because teammate Nesta Carter was found guilty of doping.

Armstrong Stripped

2012   After years of denial and a lengthy investigation, Lance Armstrong was stripped of all of his results and prizes that he'd won since 1998, including seven Tour de France titles. He was also banned for life from sanctioned cycling events.

The Cubs Win

2016   For the first time since 1908, the Chicago Cubs won the World Series in 2016, beating the Cleveland Indians. The Series was widely considered the best ever played. The San Francisco Giants won the World Series three times in the decade, and the Boston Red Sox clinched it twice.

Goodbye, Ali

2016   Often regarded as the greatest heavyweight boxer of all time, Muhammad Ali died in June 2016 at the age of seventy-four after a long battle with Parkinson's syndrome. Named by *Sports Illustrated* in

1999 as the "Sportsman of the Century," Ali was the first fighter to win the world heavyweight championship on three separate occasions.

Golden State Warriors

2019   The NBA was dominated in the 2010s by the Golden State Warriors, who competed in five NBA Finals, winning three of them. But the most famous player of the decade was LeBron James of the Los Angeles Lakers, who won multiple awards for NBA Finals and NBA Most Valuable Player during the 2010s.

New England Patriots Win Three

2019   The New England Patriots won three Super Bowls in the decade as of 2019. No other team managed to win more than one. The Patriots were led by Tom Brady. Widely regarded as the best quarterback of all time, Brady spent twenty seasons with the Patriots, his final one in 2019.

Tennis

2019   Men's professional tennis in the decade was dominated by the "Big Three." Roger Federer won five Grand Slam titles and set the record for the most weeks at number one, with 310. Rafael Nadal won thirteen Grand Slam titles, and Novak Djokovic won fifteen Grand Slam titles and spent 275 weeks as the world number one. The women's game was dominated once again by Serena Williams, who won twelve Grand Slams during the 2010s.

THE BIG (AND SMALL) SCREEN

Online Streaming

2010   Subscriptions to cable providers decreased over the decade as consumers turned to cheaper online streaming services such as Amazon Prime, Netflix, and Hulu.

Animated Films

2013   Animated films were box office leaders throughout the decade with the records constantly tumbling. *Toy Story 3* in 2010 was the highest-grossing animated film of all time, only to be beaten by *Frozen* in 2013 (which is now third). *Toy Story 4* in 2019 also exceeded its predecessor to become the sixth-highest grossing, while *Minions* in 2015 is in fifth place. The 2018 film *Incredibles 2* is in fourth place, with *Frozen II* from 2019 in second place. Also from 2019, *The Lion King* (remake) is the highest-grossing animated film of all time, bringing in almost $1.7 billion.

It

2017   The 2017 film *It*, based on the Stephen King book of the same name, became the highest-grossing horror film of all time, bringing in $700 million at the box office.

Superheroes

2019   Like the decade before, superhero films led the box office during the 2010s, particularly those based on the comic books by Marvel. *Avengers: Endgame* in 2019 grossed over $2.7 billion, making it the second highest-grossing film of all time.

Joker

2019   The 2019 film *Joker*, for which Joaquin Phoenix won the Academy Award for Best Actor, became the first R-rated film to gross over $1 billion.

Reality TV

2019   Reality series were popular on television during the decade, with *The Bachelor* franchise continuing to rate highly. *Kitchen Nightmares*, *America's Got Talent*, *American Idol*, and *The Voice* were other well-watched shows.

Best Picture

2019   The Academy Award for Best Picture throughout the decade went to the following films (in order): *The King's Speech*, *The Artist*, *Argo*, *12 Years a Slave*, *Birdman or (The Unexpected Virtue of Ignorance)*, *Spotlight*, *Moonlight*, *The Shape of Water*, *Green Book*, and *Parasite*.

Drama Series

2019   Drama series continued their popularity during the 2010s, with *Breaking Bad* (which ended in 2013), its spin-off *Better Call Saul* (which began in 2015), *The Walking Dead* (2010), *The Blacklist* (2013), *Sons of Anarchy* (which ended in 2014), and *Game of Thrones*, which ran from 2011 to 2019, the most popular in the genre.

The Big Bang Theory

2019   Sitcoms remained popular on television throughout the decade, with *Two and a Half Men* continuing its success after Charlie Sheen was fired for publicly denouncing Chuck Lorre, the show's producer. Other shows such as *The Office*, *It's Always Sunny in Philadelphia*, and *How I Met Your Mother* also had success. But it was

The Big Bang Theory, which ran throughout the decade and ended in 2019, that was the number one sitcom in the United States.

Robin Williams and Others Depart

2019   The decade saw the deaths of many celebrated actors, including Tony Curtis, aged eighty-five, and Gary Coleman, forty-two (2010); Elizabeth Taylor, seventy-nine (2011); Andy Griffith, eighty-six (2012); James Gandolfini, fifty-one (2013); Mickey Rooney, ninety-three, and Robin Williams, sixty-three (2014); Gene Wilder, eighty-three, and Debbie Reynolds, eighty-four, and her daughter Carrie Fisher, sixty (2016); Adam West of *Batman* fame, eighty-eight, Roger Moore, eighty-nine, and Mary Tyler Moore, eighty (2017); Burt Reynolds, eighty-two (2018); and Doris Day, ninety-seven (2019).

IT'S JUST BUSINESS

iPad

2010   Apple released the iPad computer tablet in 2010. Within months it became the best-selling technological product in history and paved the way for other tablets.

Bitcoin and Cryptocurrency

2010   While it began in 2009, by the 2010s Bitcoin had become very popular, with many other decentralized digital currencies also taking hold.

Instagram

2010   Instagram, the photo-sharing social networking site, was launched in 2010. The first photo posted was of a dog, and the site now has over 500 million users worldwide.

Goodbye, Steve Jobs

2011   Cofounder of Apple Inc., Steve Jobs, died at his Californian home in October 2011 at the age of fifty-six. He died of respiratory arrest related to pancreatic cancer.

Murdoch and News of the World

2011   After 168 years in print, the British *News of the World* newspaper closed down in 2011 in the wake of a scandal in which employees of the paper were accused of phone hacking and police bribery.

Google Chrome

2012   Google Chrome became the most used web browser in the world in 2012, overtaking Internet Explorer.

Amazon Echo

2014   Featuring the voice-recognition software "Alexa," the Amazon Echo voice-based digital assistant was launched in 2014.

Playboy Hugh Bows Out

2017   American magazine publisher and founder of *Playboy* Hugh Hefner died in 2017 at the Playboy Mansion, aged ninety-one. The first issue of *Playboy* magazine in 1953 featured Marilyn Monroe.

Cashless Society

2019   The decade saw an increasing move to a cashless society, with non-cash transactions dominating. Many banks no longer conducted cash transactions, and with the onset of the COVID-19 pandemic, cash, thought to be a means of transmitting the disease, became frowned upon or not accepted in many places.

Minecraft

2019   Dominated by Sony, Microsoft, and Nintendo, the video game industry continued to boom throughout the 2010s. Developed by Mojang Studios, *Minecraft* became the best-selling video game of all time in 2019, with over 238 million sold. Mojang was bought by Microsoft in 2014 for $2.5 billion.

IN INFAMY

Volcano in Iceland

2010   A massive ash cloud following the eruption of Iceland's Eyjafjallajökull volcano spread across Europe, resulting in the cancellation of 95,000 plane flights.

Deepwater Horizon

2010   When United States' oil rig Deepwater Horizon exploded and sank in 2010, four million barrels of oil polluted the sea, devastating marine life.

Haiti Earthquake

2010   A relatively modest earthquake measuring 7 on the Richter scale, the Haiti earthquake devastated the weak buildings of the island, resulting in more than 230,000 deaths.

Earthquake in Chile

2010   An 8.8-magnitude earthquake in Chile triggered a tsunami in the Pacific and killed 497 people. It is one of the biggest earthquakes in history.

Chilean Miners

2010   Following the collapse of the roof in a gold and copper mine in Chile, thirty-three miners were trapped. They remained underground for sixty-nine days before eventually being rescued.

Super Outbreak

2011   Two tornado outbreaks occurred in the United States in 2011. The first killed 360 people across six states, making it one of the deadliest tornado outbreaks in American history. The second, just one month later, killed 161 people, mostly in Joplin, Missouri.

Drought in California

2011   The year 2011 marked the start of a six-year drought in California, the driest period in the state's history. Over one hundred million trees were wiped out by the drought, with water restrictions imposed on much of the state's population.

Tucson Shooting

2011   United States federal judge John Roll and five others were shot and killed near Tucson. The actual target of the shooting, US Representative Gabby Giffords, was critically injured.

Tsunami in Japan

2011   An enormous earthquake off the coast of Japan caused a tsunami to crash into the mainland, killing over sixteen thousand people.

Shootings at Sandy Hook

2012   In 2012 a shooting at Sandy Hook Elementary School in Newtown, Connecticut, left twenty children and six adults dead. Despite the public outcry, school shootings increased, and in 2018 there were thirty.

Meteor in Russia

2013   A sixty-six-foot-wide meteor traveling at twelve miles per second exploded above the Russian city of Chelyabinsk. The debris from the explosion injured many people.

Malaysia Airlines Flight 370

2014   In 2014, this Malaysia Airlines plane vanished somewhere between Kuala Lumpur and Beijing. All 239 people on board were presumed dead. It wasn't until 2015 that the first remains of the aircraft were found when they washed ashore on Reunion Island in the Indian Ocean.

Stampede in Mina

2015   A stampede during the annual Hajj pilgrimage in Mina, Mecca, killed over two thousand people. The cause of the stampede was disputed and increased tensions between Saudi Arabia and Iran.

Data Breach

2015   In 2015, the United States Office of Personnel Management announced that over 22 million records relating to government employees and related people had been accessed by hackers. It was one of the largest breaches of government data in American history, believed to have been orchestrated by hackers working on behalf of the Chinese government.

CBS Murders

2015   News reporter Alison Parker and photojournalist Adam Ward were shot and killed during a live television interview near Smith Mountain Lake in Moneta, Virginia, in 2015. They were both employees of the CBS affiliate WDBJ. The gunman was Vester Lee Flanagan II, a former reporter at WDBJ who had been fired in 2013. Flanagan shot himself during a car chase with police later that day, resulting in his death.

Fox News Scandal

2016   In the wake of a sexual harassment claim, chairman and CEO of Fox News, Roger Ailes, was forced out of the company by the Murdochs, owners of Fox. He received a payout of $65 million.

Hurricane Harvey

2017   There were a number of devastating hurricanes in the course of the decade, including Hurricane Irene (2011), Sandy (2012), Joaquin

(2015), Matthew (2016), Irma (2017), Michael (2018), and Dorian (2019). But it was Hurricane Harvey in 2017 that hit Texas, causing the most destruction. Its damage was estimated at $125 billion, making it (along with Hurricane Katrina) the costliest natural disaster in United States history.

Weinstein

2018   American film producer Harvey Weinstein was charged with various sexual offenses in 2018 after the *New York Times* and the *New Yorker* reported that over a dozen women had come forward accusing him of rape, sexual assault, and sexual harassment. He was convicted two years later and sentenced to twenty-three years in prison. This gave momentum to the #MeToo movement, started in 2006 by activist Tarana Burke.

Thailand Cave Rescue

2018   A soccer coach and twelve boys from his team entered the Tham Luang Nang Non cave in Thailand after a practice session. Heavy rainfall then flooded the cave, trapping them. In an effort involving more than ten thousand people, which included pumping over a billion liters of water from the cave, they were all rescued after seventeen days.

California Camp Fire

2018   Named after Camp Creek Road, where the fire began because of a faulty electric transmission line, the Camp Fire was the most destructive and deadly wildfire in the history of California. It raged for seventeen days and caused nearly $17 billion in damage. Eight-five people were also killed.

Notre-Dame Burns

2019   A huge fire in 2019 at the Notre-Dame Cathedral in Paris destroyed the historical building's roof and damaged its upper walls. For the first time since 1803, the cathedral did not host Christmas Mass.

Terrorism Continues

2019   The decade bore witness to numerous terrorist attacks around the world, including the 2015 Paris attacks in which Islamic suicide bombers killed 131 people. Of particular note in the United States were the following attacks: the Boston Marathon bombing in 2013 that killed two people, the San Bernardino shootings in 2015 that killed fourteen people, the Orlando nightclub shooting in 2016 that killed forty-nine people, the New York City truck attack in 2017 that killed eight people, and the El Paso shooting in 2019 that killed twenty-three people.

COVID-19

2019   The first case of the severe acute respiratory syndrome coronavirus 2, more commonly known as COVID-19, was identified in Wuhan, China, in December 2019. The virus quickly spread worldwide, with the World Health Organization declaring a Public Health Emergency of International Concern and a pandemic early the next year. The COVID-19 pandemic is one of the deadliest in history, with more than 518 million cases and more than 6.26 million deaths as of 2022.

THE WEIRD AND THE WONDERFUL

Fedoras Are Back

2010   Worn by the likes of singer Bruno Mars, fedora hats made somewhat of a comeback in the early part of the decade.

Selfie Sticks

2015   As consumers became more and more obsessed with taking photographs of themselves using their cell phones, selfie sticks were a fad in the middle part of the decade. They allowed people to place their cell phone in a cradle and extend it away from the body, making a "selfie" appear more like a normal photograph taken by someone else.

Dabbing

2015   A popular fad among teenagers in the middle of the decade, dabbing was a dance trend that lasted a couple of years.

Emojis

2017   Originating on Japanese cell phones, emojis, or small pictograms used in text messages on cell phones, became extremely popular.

Fidget Spinner

2017   One of the most popular toys of 2017 was the fidget spinner, a small device with a ball bearing in the center of three rounded arms that is spun around in circles. The item was marketed to help people who have trouble focusing or feel the need to fidget; however, no evidence has been found to show that it helps these people in any way.

POP QUIZ HOT SHOT
(HINT: YOU WON'T FIND THE ANSWERS ABOVE)

1. In 2015, Saudi Arabia and the United Arab Emirates invaded part of which country in an attempt to depose the government?

2. In which Middle Eastern country did a civil war begin in 2014?

3. In which European country did the king abdicate in favor of his son in 2014?

4. In which country did the Grenfell Tower fire occur in 2017, killing seventy-two people?

5. In which United States city was there a water crisis in 2014 after the water source was changed?

6. The 2010 film *The Social Network* was based on what 2009 book by Ben Mezrich?

7. Which film star took Donald Trump's place on *The Celebrity Apprentice* in 2017?

8. What music genre are popular 2010s bands The Offspring and Fall Out Boy best known for?

9. In which event at the 2016 Olympic Games did Americans Brianna Rollins, Nia Ali, and Kristi Castlin achieve a podium sweep, winning all three medals?

10. Which American was the 2015 and 2019 NASCAR Cup Series champion?

1. Yemen 2. Iraq 3. Spain 4. England 5. Flint, Michigan 6. *The Accidental Billionaires* 7. Arnold Schwarzenegger 8. punk rock 9. women's 100 meters hurdles 10. Kyle Busch

ABOUT THE AUTHOR

Andrew Thompson divides his time between Australia and England. A lawyer by trade, his obsession with finding out the truth about aspects of the world that we take for granted has led him to accumulate a vast body of knowledge, which he has distilled into book form. He is the author of the four Ulysses Press best sellers *What Did We Use Before Toilet Paper?*, *Can Holding in a Fart Kill You?*, *Why Do Roller Coasters Make You Puke?*, and *Hair of the Dog to Paint the Town Red*. See all of Andrew's books at www.andrewthompsonwriter.co.uk or at Twitter @AndrewTWriter.